Why "People ir
Genetι.

"In classic Victor Schlatter style, we are introduced to a veritable United Nations that make up Abba's, Abraham's, and our ultimate family—what an exciting prospect! Victor's background in nuclear science, linguistics, and Bible translation, and his extensive exposure to multiplied people groups more than qualifies him for this task."

Bruce Garbutt, Australian Director
International Christian Embassy, Jerusalem

"Using his unique wit and thorough research, Victor Schlatter has written another gem. *Genetically Modified Prophecies* takes one on a literary journey around the globe with one thought in mind: He has put eternity in their hearts! This is a thought-provoking work and a joy from cover to cover. I believe Abba is pleased!"

Rev. Gary Cristofaro, Senior Pastor, First Assembly of God
Melbourne, Florida

"In *Genetically Modified Prophecies* Victor Schlatter approaches a sensitive topic with the disciplines of a scientist and Bible translator. His analytical and alliterative style, with a healthy application of literary sarcasm, challenges the reader to think outside the box.

"*Genetically Modified Prophecies* probes into the unknown, unspoken, and underdeveloped details of the Abrahamic Covenant, the very foundation of biblical redemption as God metaphorically promised Abraham's seed as numerous as 'the Genesis 22:17 stars of the heavens, and as the sand that is on the seashore.'

"By cleverly combining scriptural clues with anecdotal evidence, one is forced to contemplate further the magnificence of our Creator and just how the final redemption may well look. One thing is for sure, we were all created in His image, so will there be something more? Will there be a 'modified' genetic link to truly unite the peoples of this earth as a united '*mishpochah*'? Enjoy the ride and open your mind as you consider this interesting perspective on Kingdom restoration."

Rabbi Frank Lowinger, Congregation Brith Hadoshah, Buffalo, NY
President (Retired), Messianic Jewish Alliance of America

"My good friend Victor Schlatter's white hair and beard belie his youthful zest. He devotes every waking moment to God's work, putting into action the ancient sages' wisdom of 'You are not required to complete the task, but you are not exempt from it.'

"As he always was, Victor is ahead of the pack as he reveals in this seminal work what seems to be God's plan for the end of days. While others are busy downloading apps for their iPhones, Victor peers into the Bible and the headlines and provides hypotheses about Judah and Ephraim and how they may come—and ARE coming!—together in God's finale. After it's all over, everyone will recognize it. Read Victor's book and get a glimpse of the coming attractions!"

Gidon Ariel, Director, Root Source and the Holy Land Bible Bee: www.HolyLandBibleBee.com
Founder of the Facebook group "Jews Who Love Christians Who Love Jews (And the Christians Who Love Them)"

"Yeshua tells us that 'no man knows the day or the hour,' but when we see the signs, lift up your heads for your redemption draws near, a redemption that is rooted in the Abrahamic Covenant. In Victor Schlatter's book *Genetically Modified Prophecies,* you will find a whole new universe of ideas concerning how when all is said and done, the Creator God will reveal the actual genealogy of the redeemed."

Rev. Dr. Robert Stearns
Executive Director, Eagles' Wings, Clarence, NY

"Victor Schlatter knows that it is only the Father's Holy Spirit that will ultimately direct the destiny of His people. *Genetically Modified Prophecies* is based on an encouraging theme of understanding the times that we are living in. Frequently observing and meeting Jews on aircraft heading back to Israel after leaving their jobs and livelihood in New York City excites my heart in seeing that we are living in a day and age where it is evident that much prophecy has come to pass, with even much more about to happen. Whatever you take from this book, keep your eyes on Abba."

Nick Vujicic, Global Motivator and Evangelist, Founder and President of LifewithoutLimbs.org, whose birth with neither arms nor legs has been transformed into a monumental worldwide message of motivation

GENETICALLY
MODIFIED
PROPHECIES

Whatever Happened
to all the Sand and Stars
God Promised to
Abraham?

VICTOR
SCHLATTER

E*ergreen
PRESS

Mobile, AL

Genetically Modified Prophecies, Whatever Happened to all the Sand and Stars God Promised to Abraham?
by Victor Schlatter
Copyright © 2012 Victor Schlatter

ISBN 978-1-58169-415-4
For Worldwide Distribution
Printed in the U.S.A.

Evergreen Press
P.O. Box 191540 • Mobile, AL 36619
800-367-8203

Dedicated to the King of the Universe

Aristotle had hoped to eliminate Him.

The civil liberties lobby try to pry Him from those people who pray.

NASA copied His codes into Deep Space communication.

Religious rogues pretend to represent Him.

He is the original Architect of the human DNA fingerprint.

He became Abraham's best Friend.

So in tit-for-tat gratitude, He scattered
Abraham's Y chromosome globally from Beijing to Boston.
And became Abraham's Abba—and mine.

Thank You, Father.

Dear David

Be Blessed in Yeshua

TABLE OF CONTENTS

FOREWORD

The Designer of all things has reiterated by the mouth of His prophet Moses that the children of Abraham will be multiplied like the stars in the heavens. The information that codes the Y chromosome in Abrahamic genetics has been reproduced with each successive generation so that no matter how many times it reproduces, the intended and purposeful instructions designed into the original will be replicated with only slight variations in size and shape.

As we have discovered with the genetic material of all living beings, if one looks intently at the heart and soul of an individual, i.e., his nucleus, it does not require a Nobel Laureate to understand that Someone has "encoded" an intelligent blueprint for who and what it is. One finds by simple evaluation that each succeeding generation's gifts and callings, plans, and purposes are "irrevocable," that is, its "genetic" design varies little from its prototypal.

As generations unfold over the millennia from Abraham until today, the genetic imprint changes little in his offspring: the yearning for the knowledge of and intimacy with the One True G-d is reproduced intact. And as with the grains of sand that cover the earth, no matter what distance the progeny have traveled from their source, nor the varieties of shapes and sizes it may have become today, one sees with clarity the connection with its origin.

There can be little doubt whatsoever that when one examines the data presented in this outstanding book, one will see the overwhelming evidence of the Hand of intelligent design: that the spiritual genetic blueprint has been transmitted alongside the physical by our Creator through the lineage of father Abraham from generations in perpetuity.

Having been a longtime habitué of the unique works of author and analyst Victor Schlatter, I was enthusiastic when informed that he was contemplating a new addition to his portfolio. I was even more inspired when he revealed to me the topic of his text. As a lifetime scientist and academician, I have been enthralled both by how Victor's knowledge of the scientific process, as well as his expertise in linguistics, have informed his past writings.

As a Jew who lost thirty-five members of my family in the Holocaust, I have been captivated by the Hebraic perspective that Victor brings to his readers. And as a believer in the Holy One of Israel, I have been profoundly impacted by the Spirit-led revelations that permeate the works of this servant of G-d. So, as to the form and content of his current masterpiece, I must say I have in no wise been disappointed. What theories others might try with difficulty to substantiate, this gifted linguist and man of G-d presents with clarity and confidence so that its veracity is unquestioned fact.

And utilizing his usual disarming humor and witty repartee, Victor gracefully continues to confound those anthropocentric scoffers who will no doubt try to explain away the facts presented here through a multiplicity of backup. It is a treat to have someone with wit, wisdom, and lucidity come along in your generation. But when that individual seeks a direct line to the Giver of all wisdom, it is a rare phenomenon indeed. Such is Victor Schlatter. Please read this book prayerfully and let it motivate you to understand and to be a partaker of our Creator's plans and purposes in this last great revival of genuine faith in Him as we await the coming of the Lion of Judah.

With Great Affection,
Dr. Daniel Robitshek, MD, FHM
Diplomate, American Board of Internal Medicine
Fellow of Hospital Medicine, Hospitalist Medical Director, Floyd Medical Center, Rome, Georgia
Past Professor of Medicine, University of California, Irvine &
Loma Linda University Schools of Medicine

INTRODUCTION

As the world we once knew unravels and the prophecies we once presumed credible crumble before our eyes, it's time to awaken to the reality that the big-name prophecy visionaries of yesteryear may have zeroed in from the wrong angle of the universe. They told us as much as they saw, but after 1948, 1967, 9-11, and current global disintegration, we now see much more. After all, the God of the Galaxies has a total of 360 degrees from which to zoom into His ancient promises!

Could it have been that we heard only what tickled our humanistic ears? As believers, it should, in fact, turn out far better than the globe is guessing!

It boggles the senses that otherwise sober-minded theologians can come up with a knee-jerk scenario, presuming accurate Western insights into the fulfillment of Eastern Hebraic prophets from across the centuries. Maybe it will fit, maybe not, but certainly not always! And there is even more overconfidence in the presumption that the Creator of the Cosmos had chosen their whole nine yards of Western wisdom (from a selected omissions of text) as the precise way He was going to end the Age. Further compounding the error is a "religious" ego that has the gift of casting tradition in concrete. By rerunning their assumed insights forever-and-a-day in media modes of unending paperbacks and pamphlets, the non-student begins to think the former theory actually came from heaven! It didn't!

Someone once suggested that the Father actually keeps such revelations for Himself. Most end-time scenarios have come from a few choice, but unfortunately mismanaged, verses. Actually it isn't the text that is ill-treated; it is underrating a God of unlimited options. May we never downsize the God of Creation. Psalm 50:21 picks up the thread: ". . .you thought I was altogether like you."

So moving on to a final countdown, the following pages will challenge you to allow Abba to widen your options. It is apparent that nostalgic memories of the good old days have disintegrated to the dust of Isaiah 29:4–8: "Brought low, you will speak from the ground. . .your voice will come ghostlike from the earth; out of the dust your speech will whisper. But your many enemies will become like fine dust, the ruthless hordes like blown chaff. Suddenly, in an instant, the LORD Almighty will come with thunder and earthquake. . . . Then the hordes of all the nations that fight against Ariel (aka Jerusalem), that attack her and her fortress and besiege her, will be as it is with a dream, with a vision in the night...So will it be with the hordes of all the nations that fight against Mount Zion." That whole chapter is a beacon in the night!

Thus, may we also note in a myriad of other promises that better days are sure to come. Actually the whole of Isaiah 29 spells a bit of spark for divine intervention from the long haul. Meanwhile much of Abraham's "sand of the sea and stars of the sky" prophecies remain for the moment hidden in genetic combos scattered from China to Chile that the present prophets had never seemed to notice. Nevertheless, you and I hopefully might still be around to watch "when that roll is called with wonder"!

But the longer we ponder the prophetic puzzle for the end of days, the more we note the potential for the humanistic spirit to get hung up on the horrendous hurdles, while forgetting to focus on a promised down-to-earth grand finale in the future.

A routine legalistic recoil is "lemme out of here!" But the lesser grasped grandeur is when the dust of Isaiah 29 settles softly over Jerusalem. It's all in the Book—in fact, throughout the Book—as we watch for Abraham's Day in the Sun, featuring the entirety of his prophesied offspring, both Hebraic and Gentile. The sand is no problem, but imagine enjoying all those stars in the daytime!

So in these following pages, let's look at the potential of a far more realistic count of the "sands of the sea and the stars of the sky." Welcome to the Genetically Modified Family of Abraham!

Victor Schlatter
September 2011
Upper Tiberius, Israel

Chapter 1

Abraham's Inheritance
on a Promissory Note

Back in the 1980s we sang that pop chorus from Deuteronomy 28, "Abraham's Blessings Are Mine."[1] Some of you may remember. Others may not even have been born yet, let alone know who Abraham might be. A catchy little tune it was! Anyone remember? The words are directly from the New International Version of the Bible:

> *If you fully obey the LORD your God and carefully follow all his commands I give you today, the LORD your God will set you high above all the nations on earth...*
> *All these blessings will come upon you...if you obey the LORD your God": You will be blessed in the city and blessed in the country...*
> *The fruit of your womb will be blessed...*
> *The crops of your land and the young of your livestock...*
> *The calves of your herds and the lambs of your flocks...*
> *Your basket and your kneading trough will be blessed...*
> *You will be blessed when you come in and blessed when you go out...*
> *The LORD will grant that the enemies who rise up against you will be defeated...*
> *They will come at you from one direction but flee from you in seven...*

1

The LORD will send a blessing on your barns and everything you put
  your hand to do. . .
The LORD your God will bless you in the land he is giving you. . .
The LORD will establish you as his holy people, as he promised
  you on oath. . .
Keep the commands of the LORD your God and walk in his ways. . .
Then all the peoples on earth will see that you are called by the
  name of the LORD. . .
The LORD will grant you abundant prosperity in the fruit
  of your womb. . .
The young of your livestock and the crops of your ground. . .
In the land he swore to your forefathers to give you. . .
The LORD will open the heavens to send rain on your land
  in season. . .
You will lend to many nations but will borrow from none. . .
The LORD will make you the head, not the tail. . .
If you (obey). . .the LORD you will always be at the top,
  never at the bottom. . . (NIV).

And with about two lines per verse, we sang the lot: *"Abraham's blessings are mine."*

However, Deuteronomy 28 doesn't even mention Abraham—the star of our cast—at this point of his panorama of privileges. But the essence is that it's all totally intertwined with Abba's *family*, His offspring, and His inheritance, if you will. And we'll do well to keep this *family* factor well in mind throughout the entirety of our Genetically Modified Journey of a few new insights into the Creator of the Universe's Plan of the Ages.

So what exactly were the starting blocks of what the Giver of "every good and perfect gift"[2] promised to give to this fellow He singled out and named *"the father of many nations"*[3]? The first mention of this uniquely prophesied inheritance was in Genesis 13:16:

"I will make your offspring like the dust of the earth, so that if anyone could count the dust, then your offspring could be counted."

Dust was the initially used metaphor, but in Genesis 15:5, the Almighty added the *"stars of the sky"* symbolism and then in Genesis 22:17, He repeats both stars and dignifies the dust as *"sands of the sea"*:

"I will surely bless you and make your descendants as numerous as the stars in the sky and as the sand on the seashore."

But that's hardly all. The promise is repeated three additional times in Genesis 28:14, Exodus 32:13, and Hebrews 11:12 to Abraham, once more to Isaac in Genesis 26:4, and again to Jacob in Genesis 28:14. Eight repeats put it at the head of the Legitimate List for my oft-quoted *Two or Three Witnesses Credibility Club.*[4] The repetition doesn't leave too much leeway for misunderstanding the Most High that He said what He meant and meant what He said on this one.

But by the way, I forgot to ask if you read the Introduction. If you haven't, I strongly suggest you check it out now, or you may not fully catch the clues on what's coming. In the pages yet to pursue, GM won't stand for General Motors. I promise!

Another Link in the Promise Chain

Having understood, however, that the King of the Universe signed, sealed, and delivered to Abraham His declaration of eternal partnership with the pre-selected patriarch of a chosen people, four points merit our reflection.

If this biblically suggested genetic trail is something more than a tall tale of legends from the dim, distant past, then there is indeed a purpose in pursuing it. And the purpose is that the Grand Designer does have a Plan to bring some sense of sanity out of the self-centered greed, competition, and anarchy that bedevil some 6 billion—and counting—combatants today.

The possibilities of global revival—i.e., what our Jewish friends would also refer to as redemption—may well run parallel to an eventual awakening of Abraham's original offspring, including any adopted, Genetically Modified, or combination thereof!

The worrying news is that this could take a fair while without the Grand Planner's divine intervention beyond His long-term strategy of Genetically Modified Prophecies—or perhaps you prefer to call it Promises? It's pretty much the same.

But the best news is that all of this can and will involve mortals like you and me. I suggest that the more we discuss it with the Grand Planner, the sooner it may happen!

So please bear with me.

This is all somewhere in the Good Book, as we shall soon see, and is hardly a phony harvest of heresy. There is hope—a lot of it.

Maybe this is a good time to clarify: This book is *not* about how to approach the Pearly Gates. I would hope that most of my readers are somewhere en route, but if not, some down-to-earth simplifications herein might awaken the wanderers that the way is not too weird after all—Jew or Gentile. New is not always naughty, and different hardly means weird!

> *"Now what I am commanding you today is not too difficult for you or beyond your reach. It is not up in heaven, so that you have to ask, 'Who will ascend into heaven to get it and proclaim it to us so we may obey it?' Nor is it beyond the sea, so that you have to ask, 'Who will cross the sea to get it and proclaim it to us so we may obey it?' No, the word is very near you; it is in your mouth and in your heart. . . ."*[5]

Nor will you find some of the religious words and names that one might expect. They won't be here—purposely! But there may be a bit about nonthreatening relationships with the higher-ups, e.g., the Most High. But He's no problem!

You will find out that there have been some celestial plans—not to mention provision—that most of us never knew because we didn't know the real essence of the Scriptures. All we knew at first was religious rules. Of course obeying rules is hardly a bad thing, but it is *who* we are dealing with rather than *what*.

I think you'll catch on because it's more simple than even the way I write. Sorry! I do use a lot of the British overstatement or the understatement, which I find fascinating and can be used to really make a point. Watch for the exclamation marks!

And I also use the Remez method of teaching a bit, which is somewhat Hebraic. Yeshua used it heaps, and it includes parables, word pictures, and just giving hints[6] so those who are tuned in will catch on much faster and forget it much more slowly than those who need to be spoon-fed. Those of you who have read my previous books always seem to be back. If you're a new one on my list—hang in there. You'll get it, and hopefully we'll become friends.

I mentioned before about relationships. The Ancient of Days should be first—I call Him Abba—and then maybe you'll get to know me too!

So if you really don't dig my style, it is probably my grandfather's fault—though he was such a nice man, I seriously doubt that would be the case. You'll meet him later on in the book and should be able to decide by then!

Stones, Blind Spots, and Bloopers

I do have a few stones yet unturned, aka gems of Scripture that some of the painless prophets of end times presumption may have long overlooked—even stumbled over—across the nineteenth and twentieth centuries. It's not that this researcher of the Scriptures prescribes pain, but the Good Book gives a lot more insight to the problem of pain than running away from the hospital, for example!

Moreover, that wouldn't be the first time the Holy Writ spoke of stumbling over a stone![7] And, in fact, I just now recall as I write that there was someone who was a tad tacky when you looked at him. He wore a funny leather belt and ate locusts! But he also gave his listeners goose bumps when he spoke of the Creator of Heaven and Earth having the capacity to transform stones into *"children of Abraham"* should He so choose![8] Now that's an interesting parameter of our overall GM symbolism! Genetically modified *what*, did we say?

How many of you recall that prior to the 1960s not too many of us knew about something called the Internet, cell phones, voice mail, iPods, and ephods? (Whoa, how did that last item get in there? Maybe with Hebrew Roots!)

And how many of you have enough sense to know that the Ancient of Days is even more adept than say, Bill Gates—not to degrade that highly learned legend of laptops one iota.

Or how many of you have the faith relationship with the One who created life out of chaos, to realize the King of Creation even worked with nuclear knowledge and nanoparticles[9] before He laid out the boundaries of Eden? Moreover, do you also know He's the Architect for an even greater garden than Eden, getting ready for the reaping of a global end-of-days harvest?

Throughout these pages, therefore, we will also be searching out a few heretofore hidden Hebraic hints. It may be helpful to better comprehend that grand Messianic gathering yet to come. A bit of our currently considered Genetically Modified Prophecy may well make far more sense in happenings to come. Current technology tends to tease us, but to recoin a phrase, *A Greater than technology is here!*[10] He always has been, but we knew it not!

For starters, there are a couple of translation trip-ups from the Hebrew in chapters soon to come that both Greek and English scholars may have overlooked. Understanding some of these may well refocus our finish line!

Moreover, as a sometime scientist in bygone years, numbers have always been a delight to my academic diet with the awareness that the more I discover, the more I have yet to learn.

For example, let's consider *"one thousand"* years. The book of Revelation has an impressive discourse on the concept of a thousand-year interlude in chapter 20 that I respectfully view as accurate and inspired. On the other hand, the math mentality of our prophetic scholars must indeed be moderated by Psalm 90:4:

> ". . .for a thousand years in your sight are like a day that has just gone by, or like a watch in the night."

That means to me that we'd better not get our theological feet too deeply cast into concrete!

And undoubtedly, the apostle Peter, quoting from the above psalm, adds his mind on the matter, that the Ancient of Days does indeed give an alternate symbolism to numbers, in that one thousand years to Him may be but one mere day and vice versa.[11] And to settle the score, Yeshua advises against date-setting anyway, in that no one knows the finality of these matters of timing except the Father.[12]

From the Patriarchs to Prophecy and Back

And for my own personal searching as an ardent listener to end-of-days Bible prophecy on the radio—back in those Dark Ages—I had presumed that I knew all matters of end-times trivia by the monumental milestone of thirty years of age!

But then by the time I reached thirty-five, I found myself translating the Scriptures into the Angal Heneng language of the Waola tribe in the Southern Highlands of Papua New Guinea. However, I'll never forget when I tackled chapter 11 in the book of Revelation, with all those crypticisms like seven years; three and a half years; a time, times, and half a time; forty-two months; and 1,260 days.

I had no problem with those symbols and knew all the basic clues, but I discovered there must be a "password" of sorts for linkage with other end-of-days texts for ultimate accuracy of interpretation. There wasn't—except for my present abiding "two or three principle," which too many armchair prophets had never seemed to notice!

So I guessed that those who thought they had a "password" were also guessing! Thus, how the numerical crypticisms of Revelation 11 link to the ninth chapter of the prophet Daniel—for example—or any other of the one-off prophecies has not *one* option but 101. And I was rudely awakened to a bias of prophecy buffs who merely parrot previously passed on presumptions to substitute the pain of reality for the prestige of being heard. Ouch either way!

My learning curve on the improbability of professional propaganda—even by the "sanctified"—shot skyward like Noah's rainbow! Joseph Paul Goebbels, Hitler's disreputable propaganda minister, demonstrated beyond doubt that repetition was immensely more influential than truth. Sadly with far too many factions among the brethren—and far too few facts featured by most—as well as too many end-of-days tables of fiction yet un-toppled in the temple, wisdom wantonly waits in the wings!

It seems like some of those earlier-on end-of-days prophecy "experts" had made sort of dartboard assumptions from Daniel chapter 9 that were so alluring (aka: aspirin-like) that most all of the unwary leapt on board like lemmings. Fortunately, it has never been all, for there are those who do probe the truth from a variety of Scripture texts, as well as tune in to the Middle East and note a few possible alternatives!

In visiting Abraham's deeded domain of Israel over two dozen times over the last three decades, I have learned that the key verse for his future family-to-come is the assignment of Isaiah 62:6–7:

> *"I have posted watchmen on your walls, O Jerusalem; they will never be silent day or night. You who call on the LORD, give yourselves no rest, and give him no rest till he establishes Jerusalem and makes her the praise of the earth."*

Thus, the jury is still out on any countdown to those long foretold frontiers of faith. From the beginning of his own assignment, Abraham was never without his family and his future family at the fore.

Menacingly, in these days, the long-prophesied battle for Jerusalem looms larger than ever—but from Abraham's corner, could it more probably be the beginning of a harvest?

Let's go see what Jeremiah will give us in the next chapter!

CHAPTER 2

No Longer Will They Say,
"Out of Egypt"

So whatever *did* happen to the symbolism of all that filial sand, or all those shining stars, that the Almighty on not a few encounters pledged to Abraham and sons?

If you add up the 14 million Jews who are alive on the planet today, plus the scattered offspring of the legendary "Ten Lost Tribes" that were hauled off to Assyria in 722 BCE by King Shalmanezer, in a rough mathematical projection of the entire populace—both countable and conjecture—it gives us little more than 100 million descendants that could be accredited to Abraham. And—depending on who's doing the deductive reasoning—even if we add in all the fervent Gentiles who take the Olive Tree promise of Romans chapter 11 seriously, we could inflate that number little more than fivefold per generation.

But the bottom line is that all of this and more would never even scratch the surface of the massive multitudes that make up the Milky Way, which in turn is minuscule compared to the total stars of Creation. But look, this is just a metaphor. The sands of the seashore might serve us better symbolically for enormity, but again taking it literally would be a bit loopy. However, when you meditate on it, the promise was massive!

But literally or not, I don't think it even matters. The point is that the promise is incredibly vast, and the way I see it is that what we observe today is peanuts in contrast to the projected finale! So let's have a look in the Book of better things to behold!

Jeremiah declares in chapter 16:14–15 of his intro to wonders worth watching for:

> *"However, the days are coming," declares the LORD, "when men will no longer say, 'As surely as the LORD lives, who brought the Israelites up out of Egypt,' but they will say, 'As surely as the LORD lives, who brought the Israelites up out of the land of the north* [aka idolatry] *and out of all the countries where he had banished them.' For I will restore them to the land I gave their forefathers."*

North? What's North?

Note that I have translated the Hebrew word for "*north*"—as you would find it in your Bible—as a variant of *idolatry* instead. You'll see my switch in Jeremiah's quote above. We will look into the matter thoroughly below.

As a Bible translator for over three decades with the Waola tribal people living in Papua New Guinea, and with their Angal Heneng Scriptures now in their fifth printing by the PNG Bible Society, I do have a tad of translator's authority to suggest that in-depth research will well afford us the liberty to actually render the terminology as "*idolatry*" in preference over "*north*" from the context above. And here's why: Psalm 48:1–2 reads like this in the *King James Version*:

> *"Great is the LORD, and greatly to be praised in the city of our God, in the mountain of his holiness. Beautiful for situation, the joy of the whole earth, is mount Zion,* **on the sides of the north***, the city of the great King"* (author emphasis).

Again, in the seventies and eighties, we used to sing this blessed psalm as a chorus, as well. That's partly the reason I remember it so vividly. And once again, some of you will remember it with me.

Unfortunately, though it was a favorite tune, something always bothered me about that one little line in the psalm: *"is Mount Zion on the sides of the north."* We were programmed as Bible translators, that even if the researcher can't unravel the full meaning for himself, he must make the data that he *does* have to *say something credible* along with being faithful to the text to be translated. That is, he should never leave a concept dangling for his reader to make the final contextual decision, because the studied researcher should certainly have more insight into the matter than his readers would have!

But rendering it *"on the sides of the north"* basically leaves the word *"north"* hanging with no significant meaning! The New King James and Darby translations handle it exactly in the same way. The English Standard Version, RSV, and NASV render it *"in the far north,"* which from added research indicates this is inaccurate as well.

Variation from translation to translation says one thing loud and clear: "Your guess is as good as mine," which we were, of course, taught to avoid like the plague! Let me tell you that Hebrew for sure has a lot of question marks in translation into English, which we will see again in another example in a later chapter. And a good translator will give us footnotes to acknowledge that the original is not clear!

So back to *north* in English; it is *tzaphon* in Hebrew. And this is how the NIV handles it in Psalm 48:2:

> *"It is beautiful in its loftiness, the joy of the whole earth. Like the utmost heights of Zaphon is Mount Zion, the city of the Great King."*

So the NIV and the New Living Translation simply put *"north"* in a footnote. And the NIV footnote goes like this: *"Zaphon can refer to a sacred mountain or the direction north."* We might also note that Israelis technically spell *north* with a /tz/ but English may shorten it to just a /z/.

Moreover, a footnote for Isaiah 14:13 deals with a similar, if not the same issue, speaking of Satan's fall:

"You said in your heart, 'I will ascend to heaven; I will raise my throne above the stars of God; I will sit enthroned on the mount of assembly, on the utmost heights of the sacred mountain.'"

And a footnote for *"sacred mountain"* again says, *"Or: the north, Heb. Zaphon."*

Following up on all this above data (not to mention a bit of pressing Abba for the answer) put me on the track that *"north"* in Psalm 48:2 *had to be a comparison* of two entities—no more and no less. But none of the above translations handled it as such. The NIV and New Living came the closest with the footnote for a "sacred mountain."

I began to suspect that this might be a comparison of Mount Zion with some Canaanite hill of heathenism, but where? I found from my search a North Village (Tzaphon) on the Golan Heights, but that's hardly any pagan heights of iniquity! And then there was also a North Village (Tzaphon) conquered by Joshua in the Jordan Valley, but that's even a far lower altitude than the Golan. No help so far!

But then I did find it in less-than-sanctified Wikipedia! Just north of the Lebanese border, in the ancient Ugarit area of western Syria, is Mount Saphon.

The /tz/ becomes an /s/; i.e., in a dialect change Zaphon becomes Saphon, and this is precisely the infamous haunts of Baal worship! Indeed it was the ancient *center* of Baal worship dubbed as the Mount Olympus of Canaanite gods. I have also zeroed in on this in Chapter 2, pp. 16–18, in my previous book, *Nineveh: A Parody of the Present.*[1]

Check it out, including that Canaanite shrine on 5,800-foot Mount Saphon from Wikipedia because in Psalm 48, it was meant to present a perverse comparison with Mount Zion by the psalm-writing Sons of Korah.

Much like a negative "north" connotation-cum-symbolism by the southerners in the American Civil War and the current North-South stand-offs in Christian-Muslim cleavages in Nigeria, Sudan, and Ivory

Coast, the "north" in those days was a pseudonym for abhorrence. And the Psalmist Sons of Korah knew what they meant and meant what they said in Psalm 48. But the Greek and English translators never quite saw it! And this is how this translator would render Psalm 48 with total Bible Society acceptance, I am sure:

> *"The North has no comparison with our beloved Mount Zion— beautiful in its loftiness, the joy of the whole earth."*

What Jeremiah's Prophecy Really Told Us

Therefore my entire point is that "*north*" is not exclusive to the magnetic north in all forty references to /north/ in the Scriptures. In several references it could *also* refer to Assyria and to a lesser degree to Babylon, while the "far north" in Ezekiel 38 and 39 may geographically go beyond that. But with regard to the two above enemy lands, along with idolatrous Mount Saphon, *north* certainly is an alias for "enemy turf"—aka the bad guys—in general and idolatry in particular. And that creates *a significant twist* to Jeremiah 16, and the remainder of our Genetically Modified Prophecies.

But for all the generally accepted assumptions of those eighteenth-century prophecy buffs and onward, who would nail Russia as the culprit-in-chief of naughtiness from the north, may we consider that sixth-century BCE prophet Jeremiah was neither motivated by Moscow nor by nonexistent Slavic stratagems of conquest. But the bugaboo then as now was not the capers of kings, but the preference of a cheaper god for pagan purposes of personal perversion!

Thus, I doubly reinforce the preferred rendition that a reference to *north* in the Scriptures metaphorically signals *idolatry* in our opening Jeremiah 16 text. Moreover, may we continue building on this most valuable insight as we move over the globe, picking up on many of those heretofore unnoticed GM promises to Abraham.

The Y chromosome[2] is carried exclusively in the male gender of the species, resulting in the genes of the sons of Abraham, Isaac, and

Jacob being spread across cultures and continents over centuries. This guarantees that every male in the patriarchal chain carries a relationship that must go all the way back to Abraham's origins in Ur of the Chaldeans.[3]

So let's just put this on the back burner for the moment. We'll discuss it a bit further on when we get to a few more Hebraically oriented cultural discoveries, which we personally made in the South Pacific over the last five decades.

NASA's Deep Space Mentor

Before we move on, let's compare an analogy, a plagiarism of a divine patent if you will. If NASA's Deep Space Network—or whatever more sophisticated probes yet to be developed—can pick up microwave radio signals jillions of light years away, what's to stop the Ancient of Days—the original Designer-cum-"Patent Holder," if you please—from hooking up with the Y chromosome crowd of Abraham and offspring on a biologically simulated frequency to emit a hookup with whomever whenever He chooses?

Insane? Not quite! It's hardly as weird as what some science fiction buffs swallow like a shark at a squid picnic. Far out indeed, but that would be far out into outer space where a plethora of Scripture indicates that the King of the Universe has some vested interest in the vicinity:

"The heavens declare the glory of God; the skies proclaim the work of his hands."[4]

The irony is that multimillions send and receive heaven-hinged messages from outer space unremittingly, but humanism says this doesn't count—because it mixes church and cosmos! Reality says that the most stirring point of this probably not-too-perverted parallel is that anything that NASA or anyone else has ever invented has been a blatant copy from Creation—other than using their own batteries— possibly copied from China, or these days it could be vice versa!

But far more down home than that are the celestial communication systems already in place a bit beyond prayer. Did you ever hear of those pets that were lost by their owners 3,000 kilometers from their doggie dish and found their way home months later? How does that technology work? How do homing pigeons find their way back to the cote the next day? Or the seasonal migration of birds timed to fly with computer precision? Or the myriads of pre-programmed perfectly performing biological species *observed* merely by Darwin and associates; *created* at a much earlier date by the King of the Creation! And the phenomena—not only of intelligent design but incredible design—go on and on and on! Who designs and runs these scientific shows anyway?

Looks like we earthlings end up doomed to the defensive—except for those of us (so far) who are coded into Heaven's communication channel with the Ruach HaKodesh.[5] And then the anecdotes begin to become legion, particularly among Bible-oriented Christians.

One of my cherished classics is not Christian, but the Jewish testimony of my dear friend and Orthodox brother, Gershon Salomon, founder and leader of the Temple Mount Faithful, whose encounter with the Almighty is recorded on his website:[6]

> In 1958, in a battle with the Syrian Army, Mr. Salomon was injured accidently when, in the heat and confusion of battle, he was run over by a tank. Syrian soldiers are trained to shoot "again" any wounded Israeli soldiers. When they were about to shoot "again," Mr. Salomon noted they all suddenly ran away. Later these Syrians soldiers reported to UN officers that they had seen thousands of angels around this IDF officer and had, therefore, fled. It was at this time that Mr. Salomon heard the voice of G-d speaking to him that He was not yet finished with him. Gershon Salomon understood this as a divine call to consecrate himself to the work of the Temple Mount.

How about that? I know not a few Christians who arrogantly assume that the Ruach[7] whispers only to their brand of holiness! I discussed the above incident with Gershon personally a few years ago, and he said, "Yeah, I don't know why more of my people are not hearing Him." Simple! Jew or Gentile—they're not listening!

Ironically, Abba picked my fortieth birthday to begin some serious eye-opening communication with me. I had been a committed believer for some twenty-two years until the Father had decided that it was time I learned a few new insights. I've never looked back. So friends, communication from "outer space" to "inner space" is anything but science fiction!

Let's close the chapter with a bit more insight from Isaiah's pages in the Holy Writ:

"Hear, O heavens! Listen, O earth! For the LORD has spoken: 'I reared children and brought them up, but they have rebelled against me. The ox knows his master, the donkey his owner's manger, but Israel does not know, my people do not understand.'"[8]

But the good news is they will! I'm not a prophet but an analyst who does know the Good Book fairly well. May I predict an eventual awakening in the Third World that will be fairly free from the rabbit trails of reasoning of Aristotle and his mates? Nor does Isaiah's reference to Israel in the text above hardly take a broad brush to the national Israel that we know today, but rather *to one and all of us* not satisfactorily coded into that divine Abrahamic signal from outer space. We will be needing it one of these days.

Chapter 3

Simple as ABC: After Babel—China!

Next up, let's ponder the old cliché of what you may or may not do for "all the tea in China." Or how about a corollary of that to what the Creator of the Universe might do for "all the seed of Abraham in China"? They're there!

Jews in China are anything but new or novel. Wikipedia notes that there are reports of Jewish settlements as early as the seventh or eighth centuries CE (aka AD), but could well have been as early as the third century BCE.

But these dates may already be getting a bit on the recent side compared to estimates of Hebraic influences—which for our purposes you wouldn't say are Jewish but Abrahamic—that go a lot further back than that. Like a few added millennia!

What better place could we probe to begin the trail of Abram's (aka Abraham's) genetic trail than China? If you were going to suggest Shechem or Hebron or some current turbulent turf like that, I reckon you've missed a few milestones way back along the Genesis track.

Actually, my Bible-beagle-oriented research picked up the scent a bit pre-Abrahamic (if that's possible in genetics to include Abraham's personal participation even *before* the fact)! But in those days of generational longevity across the clans, it might not be too difficult to catch up the gene trail of family interactions even after a few—like even as many as five generations—as in the case of the fifth generation *after* Noah.

Let me illustrate: Fifth generation Peleg,[1] son of Eber, who was the great-grandson of Shem, was still alive when Noah passed on. Thus as family communities are once established, under those early-days *family reunification plans*, genes (and especially the unique syndrome of the male-indicating Y chromosome) may well eventually catch up! (And by the way, for your early Bible info, Eber, the papa of Peleg, was probably the source of where the family name "Hebrew" hailed from.)

Now to bring you into even finer focus, I found three sources of speculation—if not *more than* speculation—how the first Hebrews made it to Hong Kong—whoa—let's just say China for a tad more untainted truth! The earliest assumption was that some of the more faithful drifted down Manchurian way when the Tower of Babel,[2] Inc. went into receivership. Actually for the real facts, instead of a financial meltdown, Scripture suggests it was a linguistic loophole!

And I know how we linguists can fuss with each other on what to call certain sounds and symbols (aka phonemes) when reducing a new previously unwritten language to writing! This is what we found out in Papua New Guinea's linguistic playground, where since the 1960s some 400 analysts-cum-translators from more than a dozen nations lined up over time to translate the Scriptures into writing for some 800 post-Stone Age tribal languages! You may never have ever suspected this, but it's far easier to agree on biblical doctrine than which letters should be selected to represent the newly analyzed alphabet!

Reckon that could have been Babel's problem? Nimrod may have thought /God/ should be spelled with an /N/ (to reflect old Nimmy himself) instead of a /G/? Sounds a bit like New World Order humanism ahead of its time!

Getting into a Bit More Serious Research

But getting down to real accuracy, the Ancient of Days had had enough of those Babel-builders' evil ways and scattered them. And according to a brilliantly researched book on China that I recently ran into, the author suggested that in China's earliest millennia, she was truly monotheistic and her people lived with an immaculate moral code. The book *Finding God in Ancient China*[3] was authored by an outstanding Chinese Christian scholar of limitless research, named Chan Kei Thong. Thong suggests that this early God-orientation was quite likely due to the influx of a segment of some of the more sober-minded souls who had rued their departure from days of better behavior and had drifted eastward after the breakup at Babel.

On one hand you always measure your own fellows in a bit more forgiving light than those narcissists like Nimrod whose appetite for ascendency unquestionably was what actually brought Babel down. But on the other hand, what Kei Thong's research also recorded for a couple of millennia in those earliest days, was that the worship of their sole deity, Shang Di, was intriguingly similar to Hebraic worship and a morality as mentored by Moses all the way from blood sacrifice, to abhorrence of idolatry, to principled statutes prohibiting even the creation of an image of Shang Di! Surveying Thong's entire list, it looks strikingly like the Torah we know. And I'd say one could be forgiven for assuming that Shang Di was merely a coincidental copy of the God of the Hebrews.

Nevertheless, with cautionary critique, when someone suggests that the leader of some minor cult—or even that of a billion-strong power-play—merely represents another name for the Most High of the Hebrews, I run the other way fast! When you compare notes on the Shang Di of Ancient China with the Torah that the Ancient of Days issued to Moses, it looks like China actually had something unique for a few thousand years that finally fell through the cracks over the last three millennia. In fact, the collapse finally occurred from around 1,100 BCE onward according to Kei Thong's carefully chronicled account.

Before we let our awareness of Shang Di slip off ourselves, let's look at what we call "cognates" in linguistics.[4]

Compare the Chinese linguistic label with *Deity* from *Deus* in

Latin, Italian *Dio*, *Dien* in French, *Dios* in Spanish, *Dia* in Old Irish, Greek *Theos*, Sanskrit *Dyn*, plus several other languages listed by Kei Thong. And make no mistake, our researcher Kei Thong is a totally dedicated Christian believer himself and not a knee-jerk ecumenist of pagan practices.

Back to Abraham

So what about Abraham? Related or not—the Chinese worship of Shang Di began not a few years before his time.

Nevertheless, let's have a look at Genesis 25:1–6, which occurred sometime after Sarah's death and Abraham's following marriage to Keturah:

> *"Abraham took another wife, whose name was Keturah. She bore him Zimran, Jokshan, Medan, Midian, Ishbak and Shuah. Jokshan was the father of Sheba and Dedan; the descendants of Dedan were the Asshurites, the Letushites and the Leummites. The sons of Midian were Ephah, Epher, Hanoch, Abida and Eldaah. All these were descendants of Keturah. Abraham left everything he owned to Isaac. But while he was still living, he gave gifts to the sons of his concubines and sent them away from his son Isaac* **to the land of the east**" (Author emphasis).

Did the offspring of Keturah—or at least some of them who might have carried Abraham's Y chromosome with them—meander down a Manchurian Memory Lane to link up with the remnant of Babel that seemingly had found solace in rediscovering a familiar echo from the Most High in Shang Di? East is east and west is west. And east of Babylon is certainly not London—it's more like Beijing way, if you're getting my point!

Moreover, this is hardly to measure the moral integrity of any and all Oriental offspring of Patriarch Abraham of earliest days. Rather it's to grasp the probability of a grandiose scattering of Abrahamic seed for days yet to come—better days! Like our days?

But that's hardly the only options for the Hebraic heritage of China. I usually like to explore to identify *all* of those "two or three witnesses"[5] in order to drive the point home. Therefore, what if that early speculation of the sometime Babel-builders' eastward migration was nothing more than that—mere speculation?

Well, we still have Ketura's kids with so-called travel vouchers for Persia and points east! But there's even more—much, much more. In another most comprehensive study by E. Raymond Capt,[6] he suggests that since the Assyrians used a variation of names for the Israelites dispersed in 722 BCE, that included names like *"House of Isaac"* (cf. Amos 7:9 and 7:16):

> *7:9) "The high places of Isaac will be destroyed and the sanctuaries of Israel will be ruined; with my sword I will rise against the house of Jeroboam."*

> *7:16) Now then, hear the word of the LORD. You say, "Do not prophesy against Israel, and stop preaching against the house of Isaac. . . ."*

The "house of Isaac" was also known as the *Sakka's* or sometimes *eastern Scythians* who were recorded to have also migrated to China around 175 BCE. So whether or not they may have missed the boat from Babel, it looks like other Israelites eventually may have made it there regardless—with or without Ketura's clan. And since the off-spring of Abraham has had a fairly fond affinity for fellowship, I'd say there are genuinely favorable odds that a goodly number eventually found each other after time. That could have included even one more—alternative number four—via the renowned Silk Road from the second century BCE onward into the fifteenth century CE.

Look, I hope you don't think I'm talking about merely getting to-gether for a party or some such absurdity, but over a millennium or more, we're looking at establishing a community or communities like good Jews are wont to do. And we can be sure that's exactly how it would have happened!

The Genetic Countdown

China has also been researched as well by Dianna Matsumoto in *The Soul of a Nation*.[7] She likewise reinforces all we have discovered on China's revered Shang Di and his Hebraic reflections from time immemorial.[8] We'll meet Dianna in the next chapter to further note Japan's unlikely link in the genetic chain, so let us press ahead! Our Hebraic brethren did indeed make it to both ends of the Orient and in force—maybe four times over, and without a shadow of a doubt, will carry along a reasonable contingent of Abraham's Y chromosome with them.

I remember hearing a lecture some years back by highly respected Chief Rabbi Shlomo Riskin of Efrat, Gush Etzion. The good rabbi wistfully reflected on Israel's currently marginal numbers: "Whatever happened to us? Had we maintained our population proportions as they were in the days of Solomon's golden reign, by now we would numerically register way up there with China!"

No worries, Rabbi. I predict that when the total tally of Abraham's yet hidden heritage bursts forth from a hitherto shrouded mystique, there will be no misgivings!

China is but a beginning; Japan is next, and then Africa and Southeast Asia. And then there should be some real surprises in the Islands of the Sea, where I have been taking mental memoranda for the last five decades.

This will not even take into account any and all of that Abrahamic gene pool that has drifted north and westward, under the much more popularized "*Lost Tribes*" banner.

Is anyone ready for a biblical recount?

CHAPTER 4

Where Did Japan Get
Their Omikoshi Ark?

About a year ago, a good friend of ours who, herself, had been a periodic short-term Christian volunteer worker in Japan—was a bit excited to share with my wife and me what she in turn had recently learned from a colleague in Shintoist-gripped Japan. It was all about the Omikoshi.

The Omikoshi is a portable Shinto shrine that—if you happen to be searching for Shinto shrines—you can see all over the place there. They are large and small, grand, glorious, exotic, and otherwise! Shintoism happens to be the major sect of worship in the culture, so what's the big fuss about a foreign worker's passing focus—or even notice—of a pagan shrine?

Ironically our intrigue actually was neither Shintoist nor Christian but Hebraic! Both our friend and her colleague had noticed at some point in their contacts that the Omikoshi was outright reminiscent of the Israelite Ark of the Covenant that the Hebrew priests carried across the wilderness en route to Jerusalem. Unlike the original Ark, however, it had a bit of a roof over it. But the striking resemblance was, it was carried about by the Shinto porters by two long poles inserted into rings fixed along the sides. Shades of Sinai!

As a shrine, the Omikoshi (aka A Mikoshi), is a haunt for Shinto gods and its favorable feature for Shinto's festivals was its mobility. As our friends pondered the problematic Sinai similarity in Tokyo, it more than reinforced a throwback to them of the Israelite real McCoy of wilderness wanderings.

Moreover, their next impulse was, "We must alert Victor to this one!" It had quite jolted them to the reality of Hebraic happenings from days gone by. I had periodically shared with their congregation about the significance of Hebraic roots being a hot subject of the hour in many Bible-oriented churches. So the next time we happened to be in town, they filled us in.

My Own Response to the Omikoshi

Filled with awe to this spectacle of Sinai significance, my immediate double-take was—why did it take over a century for any Bible-oriented church in Japan to finally notice a parallel to that priestly precedent of the Israelites?

My only answer was that some of the favored flock may have had a blind spot or two in connecting the dots back to Bible beginnings. Unfortunately, on occasion it seems that some of the latter-day Shinto bearers of the once-upon-a-time sanctified structure had become a tad inebriated in their parade manners. Thus the more scrupulous mannered members of the mission perhaps in no way could connect the dots from that perverted Omikoshi parade with the sanctity of the true Ark's solemn source. Thus they immediately severed the former reflection from its roots—Hebraic roots. And the holy heritage became utterly lost to the should-have-been-alert onlookers of over a century ago. But fortunately it was not lost forever!

This significant fact should be a wakeup call for all of us. May we never lose sight that it took a mere forty days from God's giving to Moses those two sacred slabs of stone—complete with the Ten Top Tenets of Behavior—until that grim substitute by Brother Aaron with a Calf of Gold![1] It happened to them—it happens to us!

So then, what standard of sanctity might yet unravel in three millennia? Before we finish with these pages, better we have a chat with Abba on what needs to be fixed first!

Already begun, thanks to these my more alert friends, they had found and planted a seed of Omikoshi curiosity in my mind, and from there, it germinated and grew for several months.

Those of you who also know my Abba realize that statistics of probability never worry Him. So after many days of duration, my wife and I were participating in a biblically focused conference a thousand miles away—something like at the other end of the rainbow.

At one midday conference meal, we had picked up our tray of food and headed for a nearly empty table—except for one possibly lonely lady so we joined her. She was Dianna Matsumoto, whom we mentioned briefly in the previous chapter. Surprised by hearing her Japanese surname, we learned that her husband was an official with the Billy Graham team in Japan. And Abba immediately turned up the voltage on my Omikoshi search engine of a few months previous.

Had she ever heard of Omikoshi? Indeed she had and more! She had spent the last two and a half years writing her book, *The Soul of a Nation*[2]—in Shintoist Japan no less—that featured among other Hebraic origins, the significance of that Omikoshi phenomenon of Hebraic legacy. And she was searching out options at that very moment for added avenues for her book's distribution! Her book has now been added to Amazon but—also in a lesser window of her work—it is likewise now on our website: *www.spim.org.au*, under Books. We have her listed specifically under *Additional Echos from a Few Kindred Spirits*, that short list being directly under our own list of publications.

Omikoshi, indeed! Divine appointments indeed! And add to that, our Abba proves Himself once more as a sanctified collector of valuable colleagues, which features a cast of the chosen a bit upscale to Facebook! And I must add—one more link in the chain of global exploration of Genetically Modified Promises to the Patriarchs.

We began this chapter with a somewhat unlikely secular story of a pagan parade. Yet we press on with perhaps an even more improbable genetic pattern of Abraham's Y chromosome across the Orient.

Japan Joins the Journey

Beginning with Japan's overlay of Shintoism featuring the Omikoshi shrine is actually a total reversal of focus. Turned around, the once-upon-a-time sacred Omikoshi Ark in reality represented a *decline* from Hebraic-like roots into a sort of Shintoist golden calf from former times. It was the end of the line of the Creator's earlier divine destiny for humanity because a Nipponese Moses never happened to drop by to repair the ruins of departure from earlier days.[3]

In an earlier era, Japan's spiritual fortunes fared far more favorably than the current golden calf of her economic prowess, not to mention the idolatry of a synthesized "calf" of financial cultural success.

Dianna Matsumoto's research tells us that Japan's earlier search of the spiritual was minimally Shintoist although maximally rooted in a Shang Di setting reflective of a monotheistic China from earliest times. That was a China complete with a creationist concept from one-only sovereign God.

Matsumoto quotes Edwin Reischauer, author of *Japan: The Story of a Nation*[4] in saying: "Culturally, Japan is a daughter of Chinese civilization, much as the countries of Northern Europe are daughters of Mediterranean culture."[5]

The list of similarities to China as a forerunner is long. From ancient monotheistic reflections, the biblical overtones of the God of the Hebrews in the parallel worship of Shang Di to cultural concepts aligned with Genesis 1:1–2:

"In the beginning God created the heavens and the earth. Now the earth was formless and empty, darkness was over the surface of the deep, and the Spirit of God was hovering over the waters."

Compare that with the nearly identical Japanese texts as late as 712 CE that philosophized:

"Now when chaos had begun to condense, but force and form were not yet manifest, and there was naught names, naught done, who

could know its shape? Nevertheless Heaven and Earth first parted, and the three Deities performed the commencement of creation."[6]

Where did they get that? It certainly didn't come from Confucius, Buddhism, nor the plethora of pandering to petty Shintoist spirits! As Solomon was wont to remind us, "*Is there anything new under the sun?*"[7]

The Only Way to Coast Is Downhill

The freedom-beleaguered slaves of Egypt seemed to be subject to forty-year cycles of sanctity before they invariably caved into the Baals of Canaan in the book of Judges.[8] So is it any wonder that Japan eventually capitulated with flagging fidelity after a millennium or so?

But unfortunately they did. In time, Shintoism rolled in around an estimated 300 BCE at the earliest, along with its convoy of spirit deities. Buddhism in due course evolved into second place around 700–800 CE, suggesting more of a focus on good deeds and a fixation on reaching Nirvana with notions of the next round to come later! From then on, there was a modern mix of secularism that remains in the forefront to this day. Or dare we say, ". . . Back to ye olde gilded calf"?[9]

But of course, our search for Abraham's sand of the seashore is not in what Japan was, but in where Japan is potentially heading now. Looking back—much like all the nations sadly—they knew it but they blew it! So what's next?

Japan's Personal Links to the Patriarchs

As already noted, we see the general awareness of a Hebraic-laced monotheism that filtered in through Chinese influence from the earliest times. More specific Hebraic insights were suggested to have been brought in through the Silk Road, which connected Europe and the Far East by both land and sea. That was from as early as 300–400 BCE until the turn of the fifteenth century CE, when Moslem attackers rendered the 4,000-mile trek unsafe to travel.

Nevertheless, research indicates that the Silk Road[10] was a predominant route for Hebraic (aka Abrahamic) genetics to infiltrate across time to Nipponese soil. It was an early route, but as with their predecessors, hardly the earliest tracks of Hebraic eastward migration. There was, of course, that breakdown in communications during that Tower Trauma at Babel that scattered the *Builders Union*! And there were also those other specific links of eastward drift by the House of Isaac as noted by the Prophet Amos, traced from the Assyrian exile.

As I noted before, this is primarily to touch on—but hardly to feature *all*—the earlier links with the Israelites.

If you want to know more there are two worthwhile websites that will even give you photos of the Omikoshi Ark, the starkly similar layout the Israelite Holy of Holies with a modern Shinto shrine, tassels on the robes of Shinto priests as taught in the Torah, a phylactery (aka Tefillin) worn on the head of a Japanese priest in training, as well as an ancient statue of a Japanese Samurai with side-locks (*peyot*) as seen among the Ultra Orthodox of Israel up to this very day. Moreover, the traditional festival featuring the Genesis 22 rendition of the "Binding of Isaac" called "Ontohsai" is held annually in April. See it online with the URLs,[11] and examine the following incredibly comparative alphabet of a Japanese international orthography beyond the more recognized standard of Japanese characters. It's all there and more!

Comparison Table of Japanese Katakana and Ancient Hebrew Symbols

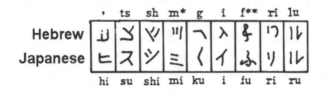

28

Thus, with regard to Japan and the Far East, we might say of Abraham's Hebraic flow—been there, reflected that! The cultural seeds were planted along with the undoubtedly physically disseminated genetics, as well.

What on Earth Do the Pacific Islands Have to Do with Israel?

However, what will follow next in these coming pages are hardly the seeds, but a preview of the promised Abrahamic tree of tomorrow. In the chapters ahead, we're going to see the potential of those prophecies to Abraham, Isaac, and Jacob that the kings of the Earth rarely ever knew and sadly, much of the Church has even long since forgotten!

We ourselves stumbled onto an unexpected if not unique response to the sand and stars of Abraham strewn across the Islands of the Sea from 1961 onward.

Most of the clues to a rare and hardly anticipated Stone Age adventure can be found on the Main Menu of our website[12] under *Israel and the Islands*. The sub-heading to that section is also our chapter division above: *What on Earth Do the Pacific Islands Have to Do with Israel?*

The following three paragraphs are a brief but invaluable link to our South Pacific saga before we go full-on into it in Chapter 5:

A most interesting discovery has been that in contrast to so much of the rest of the globe, there is not to be found one iota of anti-Semitism throughout the **original** inhabitants of the Pacific Islands...Most of the Western World has such an undercurrent of humanism from ancient Greek philosophers, we have unwittingly lost the initial biblical understanding of a God-ordained family model designed to ultimately bless the universe. Unfortunately Hellenistic logic had replaced Hebraic legacy, but fortunately the islanders never bought into the inferior substitute. They never forgot their culturally inherited roots!

Insights into the Pacific Island world view inspired a SPIM[13] out-reach to encourage this latent potential in perhaps one of the hereto-fore most successfully evangelized areas of the world. These new opportunities proved to be neither chance nor of human design. This was a call to fulfill what God has been preparing ever since He first created coconuts and coral reefs!

...You will discover that Isaiah, Jeremiah, and the Psalms are embedded with at least a dozen references to a unique participation by the "Islands of the Sea" in Messianic days.

I stumbled onto the above phenomena around two decades ago, but little did I realize then how this would be someday linked to a probe into *Genetically Modified Prophecies* around the globe!

In an impromptu testimonial to the uniqueness of the place, my sometime secular—as some might understand secular—Jewish travel agent took a few days of his own holiday to visit the Waola people in the backblocks of the Southern Highlands of Papua New Guinea—one of some 800 tribes across the island nation! After planning dozens of trips for my wife and me over three decades, Isaac mused, "I've got to see what in the world Victor has been doing up there all these years." Isaac, himself a global guest of far-flung travels, made his own unique discovery of a people with a less than Hellenistic worldview that he had never known or seen in any of his travels before. His unforgettable discovery:

"I have been accepted by people at various times and places *even though* I *was* Jewish, but never, ever have I been loved by outsiders *because I was* a Jew!" It *is* a bit unique!

So I'd like to take you there as well in the next few chapters!

CHAPTER 5

How Many Hebrews
Left Egypt with Moses?

Remember in Chapter 2 I told you that in translating from Hebrew to English—or Hebrew to Greek for that matter—we may run into far more question marks than with more compatible languages. In the Hebrew to English translation of the Scriptures (aka the *Tanakh*), we find it represents the "Mother of all footnotes," and Mama seems to have had quite a few kids! Probably the classic of all *Tanakh* footnotes is "Meaning is uncertain. . . ." As with Hebraic "*north*," we found it could mean the standard magnetic north, or we saw that it could be a pseudonym for *idolatry*. This occurs in most languages, but Hebrew seems to have the lion's share!

So are we ready for another one? In my NIV, the translation for Exodus 13:18 reads:

*"So God led the people around by the desert road toward the Red Sea. The Israelites went up out of Egypt **armed for battle**."*

But as in an array of other translations, instead of *"armed for battle,"* the King James has: *"went up harnessed."* The New King James has: *"in orderly ranks"*; the New Living Translation has: *"like an army ready for battle,"* with the English Standard Version, NASV, ASV, and Darby's all using some variation of martial display.

31

So where does that patchwork collection of dartboard decisions leave us? Back to my tongue-in-cheek composite of English uncertainties earlier in Chapter 2: "Your guess is as good as mine!" But guessing is not good enough for this translator! *Young's Translation*, however, did come off with a bit of a switch, substituting "*by fifties they went up*" into the otherwise "*multiple military choice*" for which we were trying to gain some sense. Where did Young get that? From the original Hebrew text, where else?

Moreover, Hebraic wisdom from the sages—not to mention many modern rabbinical scholars—will verify that not all of the Hebrews departed with Moses en route to the Promised Land. It may have been as few as a mere 20 percent!

Sounds like heresy to me—but *not so* after carefully checking these oddities out! Let's have a look.

The word translated "armed for battle" is /*hamushim*/, which has no less than ten specific directions into which the term may be translated. Moreover, /*hamushim*/ is a derivative of /*hamesh*/, "five," which adds a multiplicity of meanings to the mix.

Ironically, of the ten concepts of being "armed," only one applies to anything marshal. The rest all reflect the sense of prepared with, outfitted with, enhanced by, or supported by such attributes as zeal, good deeds, or quality leadership. However, when the numbers from 5 to 50 (aka *hamishim*) get into the equation, the translation variations went bonkers!

Unfortunately the military muscle of Greco-Roman thinking somehow won the day in English with concepts of "armed for battle," but that was hardly the Hebraic consensus of the sages. *Hamushim* can also mean *fiftieth* (e.g., on the fiftieth decade of the standoff between God and Pharaoh) or minimally one-fiftieth (2 percent). The discussion of the sages on the matter contains volumes, and it appears the consensus from which I could determine is one-fifth or 20 percent.

That's where Robert Young got his rendition for his New Literal (English) Translation in 1878. But for the record, all fifteen of these translations came from the same word, which is derived from the root word *hamushim (fifty)*.

Noting that numerically 50 and 20 percent are anything but identical twins, Hebrew scholars tell us that it is the context alone that makes the difference. Most rabbinical sources that I have checked go for 20 percent, while a couple even suggest it might have been as low as 5 percent.

The sages reflect that it was the English translators—except for Robert Young—who dropped the ball! Thus the Hebrew Scriptures do suggest an agreed 20 percent who actually did depart with Moshe![1]

So What Happened to the 80 Percent?

We dare not tamper with the text—nor do the sages. However, I have no such premise not to tangle with tradition—Jew or Gentile! Anyone who has seen *Fiddler on the Roof* has certainly come out with the subtle suspicion that after all, there may be a gray area here or there—Jew or Gentile! *Tradition!*

So here's one case that calls me to split with the sages—big-time! Tradition has it that those 80 percent disappeared in the three days of darkness—*that is, the Almighty didn't want the Egyptians to see their bodies, so He buried those departed ones in the dark of night!*

Please show me that one from the Good Book!

Moreover, Exodus 10:23 confirms that during those three days *it didn't even get dark in Goshen* where the Israelites lived! So I'll challenge any goyim[2] armchair prophet on what I call seven-dollar-bill theology on any less-than-biblical end-of-days presumptions. And I'll likewise challenge any non-scriptural tradition from the sages from the other side of the gene pool in trying to cover up the truth during those three days of nonexistent darkness in Goshen!

Anyway, I think we found a few of the descendants of those previously presumed deceased and done-for "corpses," tooling around in the South Pacific Islands in the 1960s! So let's go have a look.

First of All, How Did I Find My Way Down There?

As a young professional in the field of nuclear science in the 1950s, I decided with Abba's influence that I would best retool to linguistics and eventual Bible translation. Better I switch to building people up than blowing them up! I resigned from the Hanford Radio-Chemical Lab in 1957, and in 1961, after two more years of intensive linguistic and field training, my wife and I set out with our young family of four. We found ourselves in our new environment, which for the two of us now has ironically spanned five additional decades.

Our new jungle-cum-crested-mountain venue was in close-to-fantasy Papua New Guinea. PNG is about the size of California and is unrivaled for the number of tribes found within in any one national boundary who speak a total of some 800 distinct tribal languages. The Wycliffe Bible Translators are working in around half those identified languages—not dialects, mind you—while churches or independents boost the total a tad beyond that.

It takes a few years to master a new language and then to prepare technical papers for analysis and publication. There are, of course, no books unless the analyst writes them, and the languages are not always as easy as the Indo-European languages of the West. Our Angal Heneng language has over 100 endings on every verb, and all told, it took me seventeen years for linguistic analysis and then to get the Scriptures into print and published by the Bible Society.

So this added bit of background serves as an even wider scope of what this place is like, as we move upon serious genetic possibilities for once-upon-a-time Hebrew slaves, now "marooned" in the South Sea Islands—possibly on a holiday, you might guess—after baking all those bricks for Old Pharaoh!

Secondly, How Did My New Neighbors Ever Find This Place?

Moving on after about a year of phonetics, morphology, and language learning, one fine day I ran into a random clutch of PNG personalities from the Highlands Waola tribe who were always wont to chat, so I struck up a bit of conversation: "We came to tell you about God." Their reply, "Yeah, we know," and they even told me his name, adding: "He's up there"—with a sweep of the hand heavenward—"He's okay. . . ." [God's okay??] ". . .He's okay, but our real problem is down here doing deals with the demons!"

Now from the "gospel according to Aristotle," no nuclear scientist should ever be so stupidly naïve as to give the time of day to superstitious stuff like that, but know what? I was still scientist enough to check out intriguing items like burning bushes or soft-speaking serpents in a lush garden, so I did! You never get too sophisticated to learn something new—unless you're a party politician or some sort of a media monger covering an agenda! And to taper off this tale a tad—this book isn't about theological thunder, either—it's about Abraham's Genetically Modified Prophecies, and we'll be getting there soon!

So my ready reply to my impromptu Stone Age humanities class was, "You look to Him"—i.e., the Almighty, with a wave upward—"and He'll take care of them"—i.e., the darker side of destiny, gesturing downward.

And guess what! Over the next decade or so, *they did* and *He did!* Now after five decades on, we find a transformed tribe with a wholly revitalized worldview. These—my treasured neighbors whenever I am privileged to return—are anything but jungle juggernauts. From once Stone Age, the Waolas now have a commendable literacy rate, some in English or Pidgin English in addition to their own Angal Heneng[3]—but don't forget their *Scriptures*! A third generation since our 1961 arrival is now blessed with teachers, technicians, pilots, pastors, professionals in medicine including doctors, and an array of mechanical skills. On the electronic side, young artists are alive with laptops, computer graphics, keyboards, bass guitars, and, of course, cell phones! On the one hand this reflects the whole world, but on the other hand the whole world didn't start with bare feet and loincloths in 1961, and the whole world does *not* still live on muddy trails in the back-blocks of nowhere. It's obvious to everyone but the humanists and the media that a family has discovered their roots and probably even a long-lost Father!

Some statistics that have been coursing the Internet many years now are the 129 Jews who have been awarded the Nobel Prize in science, medicine, and the arts across the last century, out of a total population of a mere 14 million surviving Adolf's ingenuity! Their bitter antagonists in the Middle East, who outnumber them by 93 to 1, received only seven such awards in the same period! And this data is but one puny file I have on record on the academic excellence of the Jew in patents, business, and all manner of technology and expertise. And don't forget the genes!

But it's not all sunshine and roses. It can get you loathed by the losers, massacred by the maniacs, and gassed by the likes of Hitler. Don't ask me *why* it happens, but statistics show that it does! It's been with us since Cain and Abel, Isaac and Ishmael, and Jacob and Esau—and not a few more sibling case studies in the Good Book. So cry your eyes out, Politically Correct Pretenders of Civility. It won't work!

But my point at the moment is that it looks like we have discovered some unique achievers in three mere generations—hidden for millennia in the Highlands of Papua New Guinea. Where *did* they come from?

One particular long-term protégé of potential—born four years after we arrived—has just recently graduated with his Doctorate in Law from a quality Australian university. Ironically his father did wear a culturally "respectable" loincloth, but never owned a pair of pants or a pair of shoes!

But by now my research, observations, and amazement is largely behind me. We live in Australia and travel the globe teaching the less-than-serious gurus of Aristotle and his largely godless disciples of doubt—people like all of us, perhaps—that there are much better opportunities out there than succumbing to the sly serpents of Aristotle's adjusted Eden. It's called by some the "Third World" with a mind-set that is refreshingly freer than what we once knew as kids from the phony philosophies of pagan Greece and Rome that flood the Western World. These were the unfortunate distortions of any spiritual reality that most of us grew up with—or was it without!

So that takes us directly back to the genetics of Abraham once more. And again, this is not simply about a surviving ancient culture from the Pacific, unless we are looking *not* at a gimmick, but rather a divine catalyst of transformation. After all, where *did* these people actually hail from? Better yet, who created them, when, and why?

Were these truly Hebrew slaves escaped from Egypt? Let's proceed to probe for a few more facts.

Facts or Fabrication?

The anthropologists of Aristotle's temperament told us that our Highland neighbors drifted in from nowhere 60,000 years ago—because their "carbon dating bible" tells them so! I find that most interesting. I worked on carbon dating[4] before some of these youngsters were ever born! We've had not a few of these geniuses drift into the villages to collect "data" for several months, create sensational "studies" that no outsider could ever disprove, collect big bucks from their university departments, media scoops on sensationalist stories or documentaries, and then sail off on their merry way. No one can catch them unless he has lived for decades in the area, rubbing shoulders with our walking data-box friends who also know a few details about their origins.

For starters, across scores of Highland languages there are at least four of their common legends that could have bounced straight out of the book of Genesis. Now who told them these tales—except some communal history more recent than 60,000 years, as Greek philosophers count pipe dreams!

One classic was about the first man and first woman who eventually bore a baby boy. Sadly, the woman disobeyed her man and fed the infant from her breast, which he had specifically warned her *not* to do. And through this dire deed, the pair lost eternal life along with all the rest of us! Sound a little familiar?

Another was about a great flood that destroyed every living thing except one man and one woman who were secreted into a type of hollow tree. The flood erupted and wiped them all out including animals. When they emerged from their secret cover, the privileged pair reproduced both man and beast. Don't ask me how!

A legend is a legend to give a reflection of what was once understood for the hearer to connect the dots. It shouldn't take a rocket scientist.

A third tale was a rendition of the ruin of a failed tower such as Babel.

Finally the fourth was the most detailed for accuracy. The first of two brothers had cooked himself some food and wouldn't you know, the second brother came along and nicked off with it! The brother who lost his lunch was irate and set out to kill the brother who pinched his potatoes. The sleight-of-hand sibling promptly shot off to faraway places, but when he came home many years later, he had become very wealthy!

So where did such a wide swath of mountain-locked Islanders, who had held no cross-communication for centuries—get these stories?

Certainly the first three ring a bell, but the fourth one ought to generate goose bumps to everyone who has ever heard Bible stories from Genesis. Couldn't have anything to do with Abraham's grandsons—could it?[3] Give me 60,000 years of "scientific" fiction, and I'll give you a nice Gregorian calendar decorated with carbon-dated neutrons!

It would appear that for the 80 percent who—for whatever reason—elected not to exit with Moses, finally got fed up with the leeks and garlic of Egypt,[6] and I would guess, fed up with the future

Pharaoh, as well—and slipped out for greener pastures than the slimy Nile delta.

I doubt if they went en masse. Most escapees don't, and that the "big one" actually had been the unique sensationalist feature of the Original Exodus.

But before we move into the next chapter, which will give us perhaps the most captivating connection with the South Pacific of all, I must yet introduce one more never-to-be-forgotten student from the University of Papua New Guinea. He is Paul Ipagisao.

We don't see that much of our Uni students like Paul anymore. We taught their parents and grandparents decades ago, but now they've all flown from the nest. Paul's father was another super-mentality genius of Stone Age vintage back in the sixties who likewise never possessed shoes—merely brains!

Actually I did mentor the father far more than the son, but nevertheless, we happened to get an e-mail from Paul last month. He shared his learning curve in his e-mail: *"Now I see it—we came from God, we're going back to God."*

The Greek world view is linear—a beginning and an end. By contrast, Hebraic thought is cyclical—an upward spiral in fact, and going somewhere higher! Seems like our third-generation PNG Highlands "grandson" is thinking in a cycle like a good Hebrew should! But where did he pick that up?

Hardly from the University of Papua New Guinea, and definitely not from me!

CHAPTER 6

Just Who Was Avram Pamu?

Much of this chapter has been touched upon in several articles on my website[1] from the early 1990s on, but to maintain the sequence of unlikely genetic twists and turns thus far, we must at least restate a tad of it.

My first impromptu and less-than-well-organized visit to Jerusalem was in 1982. It was a last-minute decision and unfortunately the tour guide provided was less than pleased with the then—and now—true tenants of the Land of Abraham, Isaac, and Jacob.

Actually the UN doesn't happen to know this—or at least can't understand it—but the Good Book declares that the land of the Bible actually has *no owner* except for the Majestic Mind who in the beginning decided Eden's décor from scratch—aka dirt! The Most High's mandate goes like this in Leviticus 25:23:

"The land must not be sold permanently, because the land is mine and you are but aliens and my tenants."

So when the Creator eventually deeded the whole place to Abraham and his seed for all time, He did say, in short, to future generations: "Behave yourselves and you'll keep this land forever. Otherwise, we'll discuss it later." Therefore, I'm not going to get into this now because the current issue of the Land of Israel is nearing the boiling point at the moment, and it's not my purpose to look at that side of it just yet.

But I must get back to my own first impressions. Even though the Arab guide did fuss incessantly throughout the tour, I at least walked the dusty paths that Abraham, Isaac, Jacob, Moses, and Yeshua trod, and that alone was worth it!

Six years later, I had the privilege of returning to Israel by midway breaking our flight from Europe back to the South Pacific. Disembarking in Jordan, we caught a taxi up to Jerusalem. But this time, we had no frantic tour schedule to follow, and we saw firsthand, the indestructible face of a Chosen Nation that actually did change both my wife and me forever. The chosenness was hardly what most people—Jew or Gentile—might perceive. Hardly was the selection for kudos and roses, but more often for pain and perseverance—a beacon for an eternal purpose meant for all of us.

But lest we lose our trail to Avram Pamu, let's get back to connecting those dots. I've been back to the land at least once annually ever since those first two encounters, and in fact since 1990 I began conducting tours for some hundreds of South Pacific Islanders that they too might breathe Bible air. And they too crossed bridges of no return!

And that takes us back to the Southern Highlands people whom we just met in the previous chapter.

Let's Meet Bud Burton

As noted before, our tribe—one of some 830 in Papua New Guinea—were the Waola people. I'm not sure now if any of them were with me on the 1991 tour to Israel, but I did have three fellows from the Hela tribe—aka the Huli—the adjacent tribe slightly larger than the Waolas whose land stretches out to the West of us. The Huli language would be about as closely related to the Angal Heneng language of the Waolas as English is to German.

Now it so happened that in our some ten days of intense touring the sites, I scheduled an afternoon off so my group could catch their breath a bit as I went about my need to contact a photographer friend about fifteen minutes' walk from our hotel. His work space was cramped—have you ever been to squeezed-up Jerusalem? But on Bud Burton's back wall he had a massive collage of every photo he had ever taken that was not to be dismissed lightly and certainly never to be discarded!

And dead center of Bud's colossal collection were three young Island types[2] that caught my attention beyond anything else. Up until that point in time, I had been the only one to ever bring Papua New Guinea pilgrims to Israel. And my burning question to Bud: "But where did you ever get a photo of these PNG girls?"

"Sorry," Bud replied, "these are not Papua New Guineans but Ethiopian Jews." Astounded, I raced over to the hotel, and by default the first of my tour group that I could find were our three Hela brethren.

"Come quick, I want to show you guys something," I insisted, and they responded in an instant. I had by then spent some three decades in Papua New Guinea, but that's not like being born there. So I wanted a truly home-grown take on those photos of the three girls! (I had hoped to get a backup of their PNG features. But that's not exactly what I got.)

To my question on their presumed origins, almost in chorus they pointed to the center one: "She's from Pangia" (a district about 100 km from our PNG headquarters), and then to the second: "She's from Mendi" (the Southern Highlands Provincial Government Headquarters—even nearer to my home). But the third seemed to be a bit of a puzzle to them: "This one we can't tell—she must be from the Coast!"

They were as shocked as I was when I first realized they were Ethiopian Jews—all three were the daughters of one father! They had joined their father in Jerusalem, arriving from Africa only about five months previously.

But from the parameters of our revelations thus far, the Ethiopians may well have had far more diverse origins than the escaped—or even released—Hebrew slaves from Egypt. But overall, we see an enhanced validity to the genetic scattering of Abraham, Isaac, and Jacob's Y chromosome.

The Ethiopian connections had been well-verified for several decades by Israel, notwithstanding, without conclusive evidence of the former trails their forebears had traversed to get there.[3]

Nevertheless, the secrets of the far-flung South Pacific Islands are drawing ever nearer, as well!

And that includes the oral traditions that make the 60,000-year—allegedly "scientific" anthropology myth—all the more a mockery, and become the real bombshells of measurement. The truth of the three photos began to stir the thinking of my three Hela visitors to tales from earlier times. Amos, spokesman for the taken aback trio, countered: "Our ancestor was Avram Pamu. He taught our people not to steal, not to kill, not to take another man's wife, and not to tell lies. But when the white man came, we forgot all that. . ."

Whatever the meaning of the *Pamu* part, we may never discover, but the *Avram*—aka Abram in Hebrew—cries out loud and clear. In Hebrew, the /b/ versus the /v/ may be a mere matter of pronunciation in much of the occurrence of that particular phoneme. Abram—meaning "exalted Father"—was his initially recorded name[4] until God changed it to Abraham[5] meaning "Father of many nations," a further clandestine key in comprehending our title: *Genetically Modified Prophecies*.

However, what was it that actually escaped the Hela consciousness with the arrival of the white man? Certainly not the follow-on of those moral principles that were taught by a multitude of missions that still network this nation of linguistic tangles! Rather it was Avram Pamu—the messenger himself—who was sidelined on an unused shelf, not unlike Hebrew roots by a self-sufficient Church that would rather forget them!

So What Else Was New, Amos?

Indeed, there were over 800 Papua New Guinea languages in which to say it; yes, but there was one original Voice who passed it on through Father Abraham that somehow became bypassed on a back burner—but only for a time!

That moment of truth that was dislodged in a Jerusalem photographer's cramped-up office cubicle that afternoon, scratched the first layer of ancient South Pacific Island secrets.

Spokesman Amos kept pondering, "You know they called us the Huli tribe, but that's really an invention of what the first Australian colonial patrol officers labeled us. Way back, we were known traditionally as the Hela people."

And his wheels of reflection didn't stop turning there. The /h/ phoneme is often only an aspiration sound in many words, that when followed by a vowel, may or may not need that /h/ for understanding. In his short time on the tour, Amos had somewhere insightfully picked up that "El" was the Hebraic term for God, which suggested a trigger that the "el" in Hela might have fit neatly into their ancient ancestry. (I tell you these Highlanders were sharp, including my young PhD friend in Law mentioned in Chapter 5, and a host of other young intellectuals who have emerged into a third generation of leadership.)

Far-fetched perhaps to some, but there is much more. Identical to Hebrew, the Hela word for father is "*abba*" no less, while the same word in our Waola tribe (next door to the east) had dropped the end vowel making it "*ab*" for father, while the next tribe farther east from the Waolas, "father" becomes "*abu*." And the Waola word for mother is "*am*" while in Hebrew it's "*ima*." Thin ice with limited data, perhaps, but there was even much more to skate on. The Waola word for mountain is "*har*," ironically identical to Hebrew, while the Hela term for mountain is "*ha're*," which only adds an /e/. Still all of this is only marginal for evidence and may never win a court case.

However, my wife and I had only about three decades of cultural identity in Papua New Guinea at that point in time, but in the two decades following, we began to compile quite a few more notes. In an excerpt from an article I had published in the Papua New Guinea *Post Courier* following that moment of truth we encountered near Bud Burton's darkroom, other lights began to come on and more! I quote from that article:

> Then there were those physical features that are such diversity in the Highlands. There are the incredibly light skins that have no linkage with any sort of European ancestry, mixed together with a further spectrum of pigments from medium to dark. In the literature from the first patrols to enter into the Tari Basin[6] in the 1930s, this is one of the recorded observations that was an utter amazement to the puzzled explorers.

> Moreover, the variety of facial features has long been a focus of my own fascination. Some of the noses in the Southern Highlands are of undeniably Semitic quality. [Sadly, Semitic noses—Jew or Gentile—are insensitively derided by caricature in the Western World, whereas in Third World cultures of Africa or the Pacific Islands, the Semitic nose is prized as a feature of nobility or beauty.] I have a treasured photograph of an old Bedouin chieftain sitting in his tent. He could most assuredly pass for a "cousin brother" of one of my intimate Waola friends. Their respective noses unquestionably had to come from the same back pocket of the Creator![7]

The Black Pharaohs from Where?

I suggest that you look up the entire *Post Courier* article, which underscores many of the above concepts and even additional background.

Other cultural connections with our first three decades among the Waolas fit like a glove with practices from the Hebrew Scriptures. Mass meetings from cultural and religious observations dated back to their earliest memory.

Moreover, food was always the focus of the gala festivities, as well. From the ferocity of their ancient biblical adversaries up to those unrelenting taunts of their terrorist neighbors yet today, the classic tongue-in-cheek quip of our Israeli friends is: "They tried to kill us but they couldn't do it. Let's eat!"

So for both our Waola kinsmen for a span of the last five decades, as well as our Hela neighbors to the west, we are now aware that the feasting, marching, and those festive dances are but a whisper from a not-so-distant ancient culture after all!

Indeed much of this may be true in a multiplicity of Third World cultures, but with the Waolas, the Helas, and a million or more ancient Papua New Guinea Highlanders, there is too much reflection of Bible times to be dismissed with disdain and a denial of uniqueness.[8]

So as we wave good-bye—if only for a time—to our colorful Papua New Guinea Highlanders, I want to call your attention especially to these two closing paragraphs below, as also lifted from my above article from the August 1992 *Post Courier*:

Finally, a most thought-provoking evaluation was not from this Bible-oriented scholar. As much as we would professionally want to avoid it, one often may be unconsciously tempted to interpret data much in the light of his own field of study. However, our final consideration comes from over 50 years ago[9] and with an immense diversity of worldview from my own.

Hydes and O'Malley, the original explorers who in 1937 trekked through the Tari Basin, across the rugged homeland of the Waolas, south down the Lai River Valley and into the headwaters of the Kikori River, left a distinctive account of their experiences in the book Papuan Wonderland.[10] It was uniquely complete with even bits of notation of linguistic terms from both the Huli and Waola languages. The old black-and-white photographs pinpointed many cultural identities and locations through which they had passed. Was it by accident that this patrol crossed the Waga River less than

10 km from my current home in Waola country near Margarima? They included a very clear photograph of perhaps the great-grand-parents of my present neighbors and captioned them, "The Black Pharaohs of Papua."

Whoa, whoa, whoa! Who in the world inspired *that* title?

This was indeed a tribute to the regal way in which my Waola friends presented themselves to the first outsiders. Moreover, they made an observation as to their possible identity that just doesn't seem to go away![11]

CHAPTER 7

Vanuatu and Other Far-Flung
Islands of the Sea

Some four years after the publication of my first book, *Where Is the Body?*[1] (it was neither in New Jersey nor Old Jerusalem, but in almost unheard of Vanuatu—a tiny Pacific Island chain in near mid-Pacific), an alert public servant named Simeon Tavoa discovered a rare treasure of historical significance for his people.

In *Where Is the Body?*—now translated into four additional European languages—I had briefly touched upon the so-called lost tribes phenomena reaching even into the Pacific, including the Karen people in Myanmar, and similar speculation in hinterland China and elsewhere. These and more are again noted and now expanded across *Genetically Modified Prophecies*. But when Simeon first stumbled upon this information in 2003, he was ecstatic for the corroboration of what he had already read and knew from the historical records of his own people.

Upon reading my book, he elatedly photocopied and mailed me several pages of a pre-WWII book by one Dr. J. Graham Miller,[2] a Presbyterian church planter from 1941–1972[3] in Vanuatu—formerly the New Hebrides.

Dr. Miller acknowledged in his reports of their earliest historical recollections that he was dumbfounded to learn from those very ancient tribesmen prior to any other pre-Western contact, that they had long associated their origins with "ten lost tribes" of somewhere.

Moreover, in the Vakamai dialect of the Shepherd Tribe, the name they had given to their earliest contacts for their "high God" was *Yehova Ariki*; while on Tanna Island, some 300 kilometers to the south, the expression there for "high God" was *Iehowa Asori*. Again we specifically emphasize that these names had, of course, been rooted in those languages *before* Western contact.

Shades of Chapter 5 in *GM Prophecies!* This is a near replay of my own experience in that initial contact with Waola tribesman from Papua New Guinea, even to the fine-tuning of a hierarchy of gods. The God of Creation was recognized in each case as the "High God" while demon types were categorized as the less-than-prized bit players!

And one additional linguistic backup from across the deep blue sea to the far south came about when I met a group of Cook Islanders several years after that initial exchange of data with Simeon Tavoa. The Cook Islanders had some years ago migrated to Australia, and as I frequently compare anecdotes from one island nation to another, I mentioned to them the concept of *Yehova Ariki*. "*Yehova*" never raised an eyebrow, but "*Ariki*" certainly did! "Why, that's our word in the Cook Islands for 'king,'" was their enthusiastic reply. And thus we can connect a few more dots—over some 2,000 miles of the briny blue with an added four or five other language groups thrown in between! *Ariki* is a Pacific term across much of the region for king. And with further checking *Asori* is identical—but in another dialect!

Ironically, the above two spellings of—"*Yehova*" and "*Iehowa*" didn't even make it past my secular spelling checker, suggesting I ought to be spelling both names—"*Yehova*" and "*Iehowa*" with a /j/. Interesting— even a heathen spelling checker will recognize King Jehovah when it meets Him!

Fudge Factors and Elastic Facts

It's a tremendous temptation for politicians, statisticians, and even a few pastors here and there to fudge the facts to fit a favorite agenda. Old Joe Stalin used to say that it doesn't matter who votes, but what does matter is who *counts* the votes! Sadly, that political persuasion probably wouldn't pass the Pearly Portals (possibly even a tad lower) with Old Bolshevik Joe! Thus I actually hate to pander to his precedent, but it is a classic example. Perhaps Churchill said it a bit better when he said that there are three kinds of lies: plain lies, contemptible lies, and statistics!

Anyway, after sorting through Dr. Miller's above report for some while, and possibly relaying it myself a time or two, I began to wrestle with the rightness of the report. That is, if all the Hebrews didn't attend all the Sinai sessions of sanctity with Moses, how could the left-behinds ever have known who *Yehova* was—or any variant terminology after a few eons?

Actually, a bit of research recognizes that the probability of overlap was not really too difficult to bridge! The Almighty did *not* reveal the divine name He wanted to be known as at Sinai at all. The name was relayed to Moses in the Midian desert in the encounter at the Burning Bush nearing—but not exactly on—his eightieth year. This was also approximately the time he left Egypt on the Wilderness Journey. However, allowing for the time that Moses and Aaron spent dickering with Pharaoh, the total would have run into a number of months, and far more than enough time for the "*word*" of the divine encounter to get passed around—indeed a *key* word intertwined with all this potential and volatile upheaval and transition. The "Word" was that divine name—YHWH, the root to Jehovah—which is an ultra-sensitive issue to God-fearing Jews to this very day.

If the Hebrews would have recalled anything from their roots, that name was it! I had no more questions on the credibility potential from that point. They would have known, and the legendary account somehow surfaced in the South Pacific!

Hints of Hebraisms in Pacific Cultural Practices

And there were many more fascinating reflections from Father Abraham. Dr. Miller also discovered that male circumcision as initially decreed upon Abraham for himself and his entire family[4] was widely practiced in the indigenous New Hebrides!

Circumcision was also practiced in a number of tribes in Papua New Guinea as well, yet in PNG it was nowhere nearly as widespread as found in Vanuatu. But irony of ironies! Even though Papua New Guinea circumcision was limited, guess who pressured those tribal folks found to be practicing it back in the 1940s to cease and desist? It was hardly the colonial authorities, but rather the more "Bible-oriented" missionaries! Hebraic roots always did take a bit of a beating across the board!

Oh yes, and there's a flood of other Hebraisms in that long-lost remnant in Vanuatu that makes for interesting current-day reflections. In fact, many of these folks have become my very personal friends!

So let's look at some of their other culturalisms. Some may apply to a few varied universalisms, which could only suggest an even wider Hebraic influence. Yet others may be uniquely Vanuatuan—aka ni-Vunuatu—or Papua New Guinean as noted next door.

Gala convocations for food festivals were also mentioned throughout the Papua New Guinea Highlands. The exactly opposite feature of fasting in Vanuatu may also reflect worldwide religious observance, though it most certainly does have Hebraic overtones of catching the Creator's attention, as well.

Speaking in parables is another interesting Vanuatuan feature for a non-designated "inside circle." If you get it, you get it—if you don't get it, you don't get it! Yeshua used this allegorical method of teaching consistently[5] (also called Remez), and—matter of fact—my own books and writing frequently lean a bit in that direction, as mentioned in Chapter 1. Some people catch on—some don't! The "inside circle" is *not* chosen by a chief or selected by a hierarchy. One's own resonance to the Ruach[6] seals the selection, which, of course, will have the capacity to change with the seasons of the soul!

It's hard to say why I write that way—certainly not from Vanuatu! It's just my style. Bear with me and please don't forget to check the endnotes! A high school teacher friend from Australia lamented that he had to read one of my books three times to make sure he found all the between-the-line quips. Sorry!

Vanuatuan culture decidedly calls for passing on insights through parable-talk, and Papua New Guinea's is quite the same. Woe to the outsider who does not catch on easily. It calls for thinkers, which most of the colonial masters were not! Few had gone beyond high school. They labeled my indigenous warriors of wit with crude epithets, which gave me no joy. On the other hand, it only made it easier for my local brethren to verbally repay those puppet "Caesars" in kind, whose mentality never seemed to notice the needle!

Other heavily Hebraic parallels were the practice of "blessing and cursing," which may well be from the divine authority of the Almighty or, alternately from the impromptu invective of one's fellow man, which could well fall short of approval from above.[7]

Then there was the personal Vanuatuan practice of taking a vow that was similar to a Nazirite vow;[8] also of sending out spies[9] in times of warfare; or even lesser issues, such as women living in insolated huts during menstruation[10]—common as well across Papua New Guinea— and women being recognized inheritors of property when there were no men or boys in the family.[11] It's in the Bible!

The list was long. Other Vanuatuan practices were marking boundaries for tribal land limits that have deeply rooted Hebraic origins still reflected today throughout the Pacific Islands.[12] And one last very significant prohibition was against marriage to, or sexual relations with, a close family member such as a sister or cousin.[13] This also may apply to some other cultures but hardly all.

Where Did Solomon Get His Gold?

Next door to the north are the Solomon Islands—almost 1,000 of them—that also had been suggested to symbolically imitate the stars of the sky strewn across a simulated aquatic observatory of approximately 25,000 square kilometers of South Pacific Ocean. They are located directly between Papua New Guinea and Vanuatu. So with a name like *the Solomons*, one may well have supposed that had he ever been there, the much-married king may well have left a kinsman or two in the area to lodge his legacy? Not so! Where did the name come from, anyway?

Well, it appears that as beautiful as gold bullion seemed from then to now to lure the lustful, in 1568 the early Spanish explorer, Alvaro De Mendana, thought surely that Solomon's Ophir gold mines as reported in 1 Kings 9:28 must certainly be located somewhere in the vicinity:

"They sailed to Ophir and brought back 420 talents of gold, which they delivered to King Solomon."

But they weren't—not by a few zillion miles!

So we'll have to wait a couple of chapters more to pick up any trail of Ophir gold when we get closer to Africa! But we may not even find it then.

Nevertheless, even though the Ophir mines were nowhere to be found—not to mention even any less lucrative mines—the name for the Solomon Islands stuck. Thus, by default, the Solomons were named after the monarch who should have been more noted for his wisdom than for his bullion; and Alvaro de Mendana—the mariner most noted for his mistake—did eventually get the Mendana Hotel named after him, which is still standing in the capital, Honiara. The honor comes as a sort of booby prize I guess!

Yet with a name straight from the Holy Writ, and neighbors like Papua New Guinea and Vanuatu, and their tales of legendary linkage, one would think that a lost Levite or two might surely surface within that huge expanse of saltwater! But dubious DNA runs as rare as Ophir's gold, though it's not because the good citizens of the Solomons haven't dreamed of those down-to-earth kudos. Lost Tribe legends and queues have been as popular there as anywhere among any hopeful

Hebrews-to-be, but the cultural, linguistic, and anecdotal evidence has been far harder to come by!

Thus they possibly should never have even been awarded these few lines of favor in this chapter. But on the other hand, way back in the early 1990s I was even asked to come and inspect some ancient altar stones the locals felt were most surely replicas of Abraham's earlier efforts to approach the Almighty. Unfortunately Father Abraham probably piled up much smaller altar stones than those massive "replicas," I should guess. Sadly, I never made it to check out the phenomena. At sixty years of age (then) the terrain was already a tad too treacherous for me. And now after two decades, not surprisingly the rugged track to the untimely "temporal treasure" hasn't improved. Nor have I!

Yet with unflagging interest and repeated diligence across two decades, I do want to give those God-fearing folks from the Solomon Islands honorable mention for years of integrity in the queue to eventually get on board the Abrahamic Express!

The good news is that those immovable earth-bound altar blocks are hardly the ultimate for stepping-stones to bona fide Abrahamic family identity. The classic avenue of alternative adoption through the Romans 11 discourse on being graciously grafted into the Olive Tree has no less significance. Moreover, I understand Abraham's Abba may be a much better bet for long-term citizenship than the current Department of the Interior, which can be a bit picky. The bottom line is really who you know! Or is it who knows you?

But finally, a totally distinctive demonstration of identity with the offspring of Abraham is a unique attraction of Papua New Guinea and her sister Pacific Island nations to the prophetic reality of an Israel regathered in 1948, plus the 1967 encore of a Jerusalem restored. In observing the nationwide responses, one can hardly dismiss out of hand some sort of a latent sense of spiritual belonging. Reinforcing that relationship, in December 1996 the Christian-oriented governments of Micronesia and the Marshall Islands were presented with the eternal reality of Genesis 12:3:

"I will bless those who bless you and curse those who treat you with contempt. All the families on earth will be blessed through you" (NLT).

By mid-1977 both nations had begun standing with Israel *against* those hate-oriented resolutions floored some twenty times a year in the United Nations General Assembly by the predominately Islamic bloc of fifty-seven nations. Within the next four years, first Palau[14] and then Nauru came alongside their two other Pacific partners.

Peanuts from the Pacific indeed! But the United Nations General Assembly resolutions, in contrast to the serpent in the Garden have only venom, but *no teeth!* However, the Creator of the entire mix—the Garden, the serpent, the Genesis 12:3 declaration, and the Islands of the Sea takes note of it all!

Moreover, then again in the July 2004 Islamic-sponsored UN resolution condemning Israel's protective security fence, of the fifteen nations that either stood with Israel or by abstention avoided condemning her, over half were from the South Pacific Islands. A sheer coincidence possibly? Probably not!

CHAPTER 8

The Wrong Place at the Wrong Time

Next to the millennia of mistreatment of Father Abraham's Hebrew heritage from almost the dawn of time, no other people group seems to have copped so much persecution, genocide, and ethnic cleansing—and for so long—as have the Karens living in Myanmar (aka Burma), Thailand, Laos, and environs.[1]

I know, I know, the Gypsies, many black ethnicities, and myriads of other minorities have suffered slavery, genocide, and systematic suppression in terms of centuries, but with the Hebrews, aka Jews, it's been tens of centuries and more! From not only the centuries of slavery in Egypt, we then can also recall the routing of their numbers first to Nineveh, then next to Babylon. From there it was the likes of Persia's Haman, and then it was the Greeks and Roman's sadistic bloodletters. Moreover, Europe's inherited anti-Semitism didn't die in a day!

Amalek's venom was ever upon them from their departure out of Egypt,[2] coming into full bloom a millennium later with the onset of Islam. Joining that, we all know of Hitler's acts of insanity-cum-inhumanity. And these days they even have neighbors whose holy books suggest the flow on of fabricated down to earth frequent flyer points for every time you kill a Jew. It's written in Arabic of course! The venomous mentality is inconceivable to a twenty-first-century world![3]

So as we probe the Karens and neighborhood "friends," you can be forgiven if you suppose that they might possibly have been a bit Hebraic, as well!

And that's exactly why we moved up from the South Pacific scenario in the previous chapter to check out a few more genetic potentials, as long as we still happened to be in the vicinity of Southeast Asia. And as already noted, the treacherous treatment of the Karens has been going on for a long, long time. They too always seemed to be at the wrong place at the wrong time. The difference is that no one ever knew about their perilous plight that ever cared—or that could even catch the attention of anyone who might care.

And a parallel irony is that much like the Vanuatuans in Chapter 7, the Karens also told their early biblical Christian contacts that they reckoned from way back, that they too hailed from some sort of "lost tribe" setting. So let's have a look at a bit of their background.

First of all, there are at least five subdivisions among the Karen peoples, speaking three dialects of a broader Karen language division. The estimated population of the entire tribe is vague since they are a scattered minority among three or more nations, but it ranges from 7 to 14 million, the lower number being the one most often presented in the literature. And where did they originate from?

Guesses range from Tibet to more central parts of China, but the most realistic assumption would be Inner Mongolia. On the other hand, there is always the option that they also hailed from somewhere else *before that*, as we will consider shortly.

Moreover, the more we research many of these matters, the more the credibility of certain oral traditions comes into the forefront—especially when they match from culture to culture. References to the Great Flood are an absolute winner globally. The various Bible societies that coordinate Scripture translations of the nations confirm there has never been a culture of their worldwide records that have no oral legends of a great flood, and the reports we have personally researched underline that, as well.

The Scattering

Second only to the Great Flood would undoubtedly be the post-Babel population movements in every direction, and that points us to the origins of the Karen, as well. The records of their more recently related history show that they have long been a hunted-down minority people of ancient Burma-Tibetan origins. But that estimation has been of a most general nature.

Perhaps the most stunning specifics from even before that middle era were the parallels to ancient China in the Karen's familiarity with the Genesis-type teachings of early beginnings and morality.[4] Early Bible teachers, such as American Adoniram Judson, arrived in Burma around 1813. Judson was perhaps the most prominent church planter in that era to leave his mark on Burma, and a Wikipedia report on "Protestants in Burma" noted that Judson:

> Astonishingly found them strangely prepared for his preaching. Their ancient oracle traditions, handed down for centuries, contained some startling echoes of the [Hebrew Scriptures]. . . .[5]

The report on Judson's initial observations goes on to include a footnote:

> The authenticity of this ancient story as a tradition is confirmed by the fact that [seeming preparedness] has been found not only among the Karen, but also, with variations, among the Kachins, Was, Akhas, Lisus, and even the Mizo and Naga tribes of northeastern India.

The Wikipedia report on Judson's work and ministry further continues:

> The core of what they called their "Tradition of the Elders" was a belief in an unchangeable, eternal, all-powerful God, creator of heaven and earth, of man, and of woman formed from a rib taken from the man. They believed in humanity's temptation by a devil, and its fall,

and that someday a messiah would come to its rescue. They lived in expectation of a prophecy that white foreigners would bring them a sacred parchment roll.[6]

Yet at this point in the ancient historical records, one burning question ought to perhaps loom large. In a sea of Buddhism, how could this animistic Karen clique remain aloof for so many eons from the mainstream of society around them?

Could it be that from their presumed Hebraic beginnings they were hardly interested in humanistic "religion" but rather a long-lost relationship with the Abba of both Abraham and Noah, who—if we compare their longevity records—obviously they would have known each other and even compared historical tales between themselves? Moreover, both seemed to be on fairly good terms with the King of the Universe in the same time frame! Go figure!

What a parallel and what a replay of my earliest contact with those Waolas of Papua New Guinea! Five decades on from that first encounter, I am more convinced than ever that they were hardly looking for some new prayers or Hillsong choruses, but an old Friend and celestial Father!

Recall from Chapter 5 that on my absolutely first mention of God to a group of Waola tribesmen with *no concept of Western theology whatsoever*, their knee-jerk rejoinder noted that "God was okay," but it was the demonic forces that gave them their problems![7] And in another early account that I had recorded in a previous book, *Where Is the Body?*, the men proceeded with precise details of his name, *"Shabkakl Yinaol, Isi Hobao Sao!"* which translated into English is: "Shabkakl [i.e., His actual name], the important son from above!"[8]

The River of Running Sand

However, with the Karens, perhaps the most intriguing trail of their bizarre beginnings was an oral reference to: *"crossing a river of running sand,"*[9] which after considerable evaluation of their corresponding circumstances, most certainly identifies with the Gobi Desert in Inner (south) Mongolia. And with more unique parallels to the scattering of ancient people movements of the past, they sadly lost those "sacred scriptures" mentioned in what they termed "the traditions of the elders," as they struggled to cross that sinister stream of shifting sands.

So may we probe once more that starting point of the earliest scatterings—the Tower of Babel—in the setting of Shinar. Back in Chapter 3, under the heading of *"Getting into a Bit More Serious Research,"*[10] we note again that the highly held monotheistic Shang Di gave a strikingly similar pattern for personal accountability long before the much later mentoring of Moses. But on the other hand, may we never overlook the fact that none of this really began with Babel, but rather:

"In the beginning, God . . ."[11]

And: *"I the LORD do not change . . ."*[12]

And once more, should Abraham's chronology with Babel seem to be a consideration, this has also previously been dealt with under the heading: *"Back to Abraham,"* still in Chapter 3 on the awakening of China's earliest dawn to monotheism.[13]

Enter Stage Right: The Karens of current Myanmar.

It may be a similar story to China's ancient balance sheet of spiritual profit and loss. The Chinese eventually lost their precious precedent of Shang Di's sanctified standards of survival. And this time around, it's the Karen's sacred scrolls that somehow got swept away in that sea of shifting sands!

On the other hand, this also happened: Not a few times in the strategic timing of the Creator's expertise, He does and will turn the tables on the Aristotles and fellow humanists, including the Charles Darwins and the long lists of Caesars of the day. And I predict, *"in His time"* it will all happen once again, quite in sync with Ecclesiastes 3:11—*He has made everything beautiful in its time. He has also set eternity in the hearts of men. . . .*[14]

So—for now anyway—this will finish our insights into the much murdered and persecuted "Karen family," except to add my own personal encounter with one of our Karen friends whom I met in the mid-1980s. It was in Maesaring, Thailand, just across the Salween River boundary from Myanmar. A highly respected cousin of mine had been operating a Bible school in that area for several decades at that point in time. On our first personal family contact in many years, Don invited me to speak to his students regarding my involvement with the research and analysis of the regathered people of Israel in particular, which I did.

From the reestablishment of the nation in 1948 through the return of Jerusalem and her environs to her original biblical residents in 1967, there was much to retrace biblically; and since they were Bible students, I had a class of eager listeners and learners. But there was one young lady who seemed to sit with more rapt attention than all the others combined.

Following the session, my cousin in an overview asked me if I had noticed the one young woman whose interest seemed to overflow, and I certainly had. Don replied, "She is a Karen from just across the river in Myanmar, and she has always maintained that she was one of the 'lost tribes.'"

Three decades later, I don't even know or remember her name, if I ever once heard it. She was my first and only Karen contact. Today after much research, I seriously doubt that she was one of those "lost-tribers" that the more traditional of biblical historians might unwittingly be tempted to plug into the Assyrian track of return.

Rather I could visualize her as one of those whose forebears trod that longer, more treacherous road home via China and across the once-upon-a-time formidable—and still elusive—River of Sand.

On the other hand, what does it matter whether I know or not? One thing that I do know is that I'll see her again one day and most probably, not a few of her fellow Karens with her!

The bottom line is that the Most High always seems to know which track His wandering kids have taken, and where they finally ended up when He wants to find them for a last call Home!

CHAPTER 9

The Longest Road Out of Africa

As we should be well aware by this point of our geographical junket around Asia and the Pacific in search of Hebraic genetics strewn from Babel and beyond, our Semitic search might even take us considerably farther than the traditionally supposed trek of those ten "lost" tribes of Hebrews. They were the more highly reported ones who were blatantly bundled off to Nineveh by Assyrian King Shalmanezer in 722 BCE. And these—in the opinion of some of the lesser learned onlookers of history—presumably more or less disappeared.

Therefore, it was these Nineveh[1] captives—aka Israelites or sometimes Ephraimites[2]—who actually caught most of the attention over the centuries as displaced refugees. Much has been made out of their demise, as well as the mystery of their somewhat elusive relocation over more than two millennia. I have and will again eventually touch on this segment of Hebraic scattering minimally, even though my purpose in this book is to dig out and display that stream of Abraham's sand and stars that has heretofore been largely overlooked.

But may I make it abundantly clear at this point that there were not *one* but *two* sets of sojourners some seven centuries apart—some returning slaves out of Egypt back to the Promised Land, while yet others, 700 years later being carted off in the exact opposite direction to a new slavery in Assyria. Therefore, it would serve no good purpose for Bible beginners to get these two distinct departures confused.

And as we noted in Chapters 5 and 6, a totally different major miscue from traditional assumptions would have been to presume that the entirety of all those former Hebrew slaves of Pharaoh's fiefdom made a single move out of Egypt with Moshe. On the other hand, those who for whatever reason might have missed the Moses-march—shall we call it Exodus I—may have had to take a multi-thousand mile Southeast Asian detour to catch up—i.e., Exodus II. And that's not to mention an additional 3,000-year sojourn into South Pacific Stone Age exile before the next bus home! But to judge the spiritual fervor of the present Pacific Islanders, that day may be drawing closer.

So in our focus on those multitudes who may have taken that delayed departure, let us all the more appreciate that innumerable hidden horde of Abrahamic genetics that, one of these days, may well afford a tsunami of surprises. This might involve both the more skeptical Socrates types, as well as the more biblical armchair analysts who *"ain't seen nuthin' yet."* Should be interesting!

However, we have considered much of this in earlier pages as noted above, and it is time to press on to new horizons. So if the name of the game might have been to flee Pharaoh, where else besides a South Pacific Island Paradise might Exodus II have meandered?

Of course, there were other potential ports of call across Southeast Asia, as touched upon in earlier chapters, that may or may not have relevance. And there are a dozen references to the Islands of the Sea in Isaiah alone—some with Messianic overtones. So there were an abundance of options beyond the Pacific possibilities that we looked at.

But after all is said and done, the most reasonable rebound after Exodus I was to actually stay in Africa! And so it seems that hanging around Africa is exactly what many of them might have done. Thus the farthest one could flee from old Pharaoh was down around the Cape of Good Hope—even though I'd suggest they didn't come up with a fancy name like "Good Hope" until an eon or so later!

Nevertheless, that just happens to be the longest road out of Africa—from Egypt anyway! And not too far from there is exactly where the Lemba Tribe eventually congregated.

The Lemba of Zimbabwe and South Africa

However heading to South Africa might not have been exactly Plan A when they started out.

The Lemba today are numerically between 70,000 to 80,000 souls and are mostly spread across South Africa and Zimbabwe, with a smidgen in Malawi or one or two other nations nearby. They claim that their culture is Jewish, which is more than evident to any visitor on the scene. They shun eating pork, they practice circumcision, the men wear the Jewish *kippot*, the greeting is a traditional Hebraic "*Shalom*," with an array of other culturalisms like the Kohanim priesthood, twelve tribal divisions mirroring Israel, and even DNA awareness that indicates immediately that they have been doing a bit of Hebraic homework.

Their worship practice is well overlaid with Christian add-ons although in some cases it could include a trace of Islam, while their affection favors Jewishness and the Jews everywhere. So if you're truly looking for the Lemba, there's little likelihood that you might stumble into a Hari Krishna gathering!

So did the Lemba actually wander down from post-Exodus Egypt? Possibly! That always remains a guarded option. An estimated time of their arrival in Africa could on one hand be some 1,000 years earlier than Moses' departure. But on the other hand, historical data is often dubious, and there are no clear-cut dates to confirm it one way or the other. Nor is there any biblical genealogy to even reinforce a good guess.

There is, however, much to indicate that they may have arrived from Egypt via a significant sojourn in Yemen from a select site called Senna, as probed and recorded by Professor Tudor Parfitt from the Center for Genetic Anthropology, University College London. In a personal fascination of mine, Parfitt also did a bit of genetic testing in southwest Papua New Guinea but during a different era. Our trails unfortunately never did happen to cross.

However, Parfitt's work in Yemen does seem quite significant,[3] but cannot conclusively confirm whether or not the Lemba—quite apart from Jacob's trek into Egypt on the famine trail—may have much earlier taken a straight shot south from Canaan to Yemen, or whether or not the Lemba may have been an unlisted legacy from Jacob's loins that surfaced during the slavery.

It wouldn't have taken many trekkers, then, to multiply to tens of thousands today. So they well may have also had a few centuries stopover in Egypt to give a grudging hand to Pharaoh with a tad of forced labor. Thus both Yemen direct and Yemen via Goshen[4] does remain an option.

One interesting sideline was a young Lemban lady—a doctor actually—who gave a speech not long ago at the Zionist Luncheon Club in Johannesburg on the brilliant history of her people. One possible verbal blooper, however, was that someone had opined that an original and perhaps more nostalgic Senna than Parfitt's scenario, might have been rooted initially in Judea just a bit north of Jericho in the Jordan Valley. Now Jericho *is* in the Jordan Valley, but Judea is not! Other than that, everything may have connected, except whether the Senna in Yemen was a first time feature or a Judean rerun? The jury is still out.

Further research reckons that from Yemen—if it was Yemen—they further migrated over the centuries via Mozambique. Once in East Africa, some reported that the migration split, some going north to Ethiopia—which we will look at later—and the others southward through Kenya, then Tanzania, and on to Central Zimbabwe, where a large part of the Lemba tribe remain today.

Another major facet of deep interest upon the Lemba passage into Zimbabwe, however, was a discovery by Portuguese traders in the early sixteenth century of the enormous ruins of an ancient, colossal stone complex of World Heritage significance today. It comprised a small city you might say, which has since become known to the Western world as *Greater Zimbabwe*.[5] The Lemba were there, but did they build it—or have a hand in building it?

They do maintain that they were indeed involved, and artifacts among the ruins suggest that this was probably correct. Moreover, evidence of skilled miners and metal workers in the complex, and the renown of Lemba ability among neighboring tribes for their expertise in these crafts attest all the more strongly to their connection. And there was time. En route from Yemen or even other stopovers, could have afforded a duration of up to two millennia. They eventually moved on, even yet again—at least most of them—as far as South Africa.

Moreover, the myriad of reports and the variation among them adds other ideas, as well, which may more or less prove that tracking the Lemba down the East African coast must have been Hebraic from the onset. Tradition has it that if you have two Jews, you'll have three opinions, so there you go!

Additional suggestion of Hebraic contact is that Solomon, as well, came down into these parts centuries after the Exodus, looking for Ophir and its fabled gold mines.[6] Scripture doesn't tell us exactly where Ophir happened to be, but the gold they brought back was weighed in metric tons instead of mini-carats! Nor do we know whether he headed straight for South Africa or perhaps prospected in Yemen and parts of East Africa—where gold had reportedly glittered—before heading farther south. But the bottom line today is there *is* the Abrahamic Y chromosome among the Lemba.[7]

And that would hardly have been conclusive to be from Solomon himself—though he is reported in secular literature to have fathered a son, Menelik, from the Queen of Sheba in Ethiopia. Scripture reports as well that he had not a few other relationships in those parts that would have influenced the genetics of Ham.[8] For that matter, even a Kohen[9] or two may have been included in the prospecting party for more theological purposes. Furthermore, for a foray that far, it could have taken quite a few years and a goodly number of fellow travelers. And perhaps beyond the vested social interests of Solomon, even a few other friendships-cum-family may have been established for permanent settlement!

Which possibility then brings us directly back to Lemba culture. A man may marry a non-Lemba wife if she pledges to become an observant Lemba but not in reverse. The Lemba lass must not marry a non-Lemba outsider, lest she fracture the faith. Sound familiar? Yet our final focus is that we're not so much interested in Ophir's goldmines or Senna's sophisticated settlements, or even whether it posed a somewhat shady scenario, or kosher[10] all the way! Rather I'd like to estimate how far and how wide the Y chromosome of Abraham and family were actually scattered.

This is hardly because I am insensitive to the implications of the social scene. The Most High has ways and means to right the wrongs of history. But it's because I suspect that this same Ancient of Days may also have some better than supposed amazing plans of His own for a Grand Finale.

Let's look some more.

The Sabbath Keepers of West and Central Africa

Thus, leaving the genetically laden Lemba of Hebraic heritage, let us press on to see what else of Abrahamic interest we might find in West and Central Africa that's significant.

Charles E. Bradford, author of **Sabbath Roots: The African Connection**,[11] gives us some amazing research into his volume of African sensitivity to things spiritual.

Bradford notes:

The Sabbath Legacy of Ethiopians is well known, but the Sabbath legacy of many other African tribes in Central and West Africa are being uncovered and discovered through biblical, historical, archeological (e.g., inscriptions on ancient tombstones), ethnographical, anthropological, geographical, scientific and not least of all genetic evidences. The phenomenal discoveries found through these areas of discipline have confirmed the Hebraic origins and Sabbath legacy of many African tribes, a fact always known and acknowledged by

Africans themselves—especially in many of their oral histories. The available research uncovered so far gives strong testimony to the primacy of the Sabbath in Africa.[12]

A feature that Western Christianity has had limited insight into, is that when early second- and third-century Christianity began edging into Africa, not all was totally new—sort of like my newfound Waola friends back in the 1960s. They knew that the Awesome One had an abode above—actually they had a name for Him—even though they were not all that privy to His particulars nor His perks. Fortunately they did pick up on all of that in a hurry.[13]

One other thing that was unique, however, was that the new regulations from Rome had to first get the parishioners reprogrammed for the proper day to pray! As we noted from Bradford that his research, along with that from a host of others, indicated that prior to Constantine, Sabbath keeping of some form had been of long-standing acceptance in Central and West Africa. We might find that very interesting!

Being of an analytical mind, I'm now wondering if they got their Sabbath sensitivities from Solomon's many marital meanderings over a millennium of bygone days, or was it from Jeremiah and the Jerusalem refugees[14] who fled when the Babylonians razed the Temple in the sixth century BCE? Or could it have been passed on by the isolated incident of the Ethiopian eunuch from New Testament times,[15] or was it even the possibility of the universal *"eternity in their hearts"* concept of Ecclesiastes 3:11? Or was it all of the above and more?

Regardless wherever or whenever early-days Africa picked up honoring the original Sabbath, a less-than-Jew-loving Constantine quashed it in a hurry!

Exodus III: The Ethiopians Go Home

Recognizing the Hebraic ethnicity of the Ethiopians and their homeward departure is now a bit of an epilogue.

The earliest presumed reference to "*Beta Israel*" was found in the diary of Eldad Hadani in the ninth century and is the identity claimed by the Ethiopian Jews. "Beta" is derived from *Beit*, the Hebraic word for house, i.e. the "House of Israel," which roots they claimed and practiced, therefore which is the term recognized and used to this day. Much discussion ensued over the centuries, and by the turn of the twentieth century, Rabbis from forty-four nations ruled the Jews of Ethiopia to be authentic Jews with an even deepened identity being agreed that their origin was from the tribe of Dan.

Bringing them home to Israel has long since been underway.[16] Between 1977 and 1984 some 8,000 Ethiopian Jews were secretly brought to Israel by various covert arrangements. From November 1984 through January 1985 another 6,500 were flown back to Israel in the massive airlift code named Operation Moses, and again in May 1991 in a mere thirty-six hours, another massive uplift of 14,324 Jews, dubbed Operation Solomon, were flown home to Israel. And finally, in June of 2011 the final contingent of 8,700 Falash Mura[17] Ethiopians were cleared to come home to Israel under the Law of Return at a scheduled rate of about 2,400 per year. By 2015 it should be history.

We now know where the Ethiopian gene pool has surfaced—it never was a problem to Abba anyway! But my purpose in these pages never was to count the Jews on their own turf but to probe the probabilities where all the stars and sand of promise might present themselves once the Most High Himself decides to take His own roll call.

The Ethiopians—aka Abyssinians—had been a spiritual ensign of Africa for centuries, and today Africa's loss is Israel's gain. As they both face a new era, I found as I researched that the remaining investments in Abraham's genetic scattering in Africa must be enormous! We merely have looked at those Lemba in the south and Ethiopia in the Sub-Sahara central-east. But the nations of somewhat lower profile sandwiched in between with their Sabbath-cum-Hebraic orientation are massive—Nigeria, Ghana, Kenya, Congo, Gabon, and many more! As we approach the end of our book—and the end of the Age—may we pay particular attention to the next step in what has become known as the Third World.

So as we close with the Hebraic overtones from Harare to Addis Ababa with an eye on what is to happen next, let us also keep the other eye on one alternate issue intertwined with both the *Lemba* and the *Ethiopians*, not to mention the Temple Mount. Where actually is that Ark of the Covenant?

Hark, Hark, Who's Got the Ark?

Well, actually, there are four claims on the table.

The Lemba say they had it when they coursed through Yemen, or lost it, or broke it but still have part of it. Or perhaps it was a replica of it? Tudor Parfitt, whom we met before, claims he found a bit of it—or was it a cover for it?—in a dusty, deserted storeroom of the Harare Museum of Human Science in Zimbabwe.[18] Looks like the ice is getting thinner, so we better go skating somewhere else!

Back to the claim table—the Ethiopians are next. The Ethiopian Orthodox Church of Our Lady Mary of Zion declares that it is being carefully guarded in the town of Axum some 400 miles north of Addis Ababa, by a clutch of virgin priests who have vowed never to leave the grounds on pain of death, and that presumably includes the odds on ever showing it to anyone else.

But how did it ever get to Axum? One option is that the refugees who fled Jerusalem when the Babylonians razed the Temple in the sixth century BCE brought it with them, which is highly unlikely, but not as unlikely as runaway Jews leaving it in the custody of even the most pious of Christian priests!

Another one is that Solomon's son Menelik, born to him by the Queen of Sheba, carted it to the church site when no one was looking. I hate to be cynical—although I may be on occasion—and this happens to be one of those days!

Let's go back to Jerusalem!

This brings us a bit closer to where the sanctified repository of

Sinai's secrets might have been hidden away for centuries on end. In 70 CE the beastly Roman army was advancing en masse, and the most sacred treasure imaginable to be kept out of the hands of pagan Roman mockery was that hallowed Ark. What to do? The most logical hideaway was in one of the ingenious crypts beneath the Temple.

Since 1967 the Jews have been back into the midst of their holiest heritage. But at the answerability to causing WWIII, no serious digging has been done. In all empathy with the antiquities experts, we may have to wait a day or so longer. Nevertheless, perhaps this is the most reasonable speculation so far?

But there's one more. In the second book of Maccabees—one of the disputed books of Scripture, which is actually the nearest in Hebraic history to the rest of the canon of the Good Book—there is a bit of reference to the identical dilemma. The Roman pagans are approaching! What do we do with this super-sanctified safe box for Sinai's irreplaceable stone tablets?

An obviously different Jeremiah from the renowned prophet—though he must have been a priest if he dared touch the Ark—led a group to a cave reportedly identified as being in the Judean hills. They hid the holy repository in a desert cave and covered the entrance with stones. If you have ever seen these illusive limestone caves or crypts, you'd get the picture. The text in 2 Maccabees 2:5–7 went like this:

Jeremiah came and found a cave-dwelling, and he brought there the tent and the ark and the altar of incense; then he sealed up the entrance. Some of those who followed him came up intending to mark the way, but could not find it. When Jeremiah learned of it, he rebuked them and declared: "The place shall remain unknown until God gathers his people together again and shows his mercy."

To me this seems as credible as secreting it under the Temple Mount and moreover has the backing of what many groups recognize as legitimate Jewish history—i.e., Scripture.

But before we leave this chapter—with our apologies to hopeful

Ethiopian guardians of holy things included—that other Jeremiah, aka the weeping Prophet, also left us a highly prized book of prophecy in our Bibles. He did say one other thing some six centuries before that Ark of the Covenant had ever gone missing. In Jeremiah 3:16 he wrote:

> *"In those days, when your numbers have increased greatly in the land," declares the LORD, "men will no longer say, 'The ark of the covenant of the LORD.' It will never enter their minds or be remembered; it will not be missed, nor will another one be made."*

Maybe that's the answer and maybe—just maybe—when the Ancient of Days sends out His roll call to tally Abraham's final stars and sand for the Homecoming Parade, it is just going to be so satisfying we'll never miss Sinai's sentimentality. Just like the good prophet proposed!

CHAPTER 10

America Was Discovered
by Colombo Ben[1] Who?

Undoubtedly the year 1492 signals to the majority of Americans the much acclaimed anniversary of Christopher Columbus's initial arrival onto the shores of the West Indies—it wasn't the North American continent per se but close enough to dignify the date.

Except for the new little kid in the class who never could catch on to history not to mention numbers! So his Grade One teacher taught him this little jingle to indelibly imprint this important insight for forever and a day: *"In fourteen hundred and ninety-two, Columbus sailed the ocean blue."*

The next day at trauma time, he was quizzed on his new wealth of statistics, to which he parroted: *"In fourteen hundred and ninety-three, Columbus sailed the deep blue sea."*

He should have checked his iPad!

Nevertheless the date stands, even though Colombo's actual arrival on the true shoreline of the new continent was *not* until 1498. Thus, the mainland arrival record was immediately contested by Italian Amerigo Vespucci (Latin for *Americus Vespucius*), after whom the new nation was connivingly called—to Spanish ears at least—*America*!

Vespucci's true initial landing on the continent proper had been one year previous in 1497 to upstage the challenged champ. But to never let the facts get in the way of a crafty rerun, the 1492 date of his West Indies arrival has never been lifted from Christopher's orbit of celebrity!

However, most other worldwide bystanders probably would never know what else happened that same year.

The Jews do! That's the year the Marano Jews—*Marano* meaning "swine" in early Spanish—were sadistically driven out of Spain and Portugal.

It should hardly raise an eyebrow why it is so difficult for today's Jews to mend fences with so-called Christianity, considering the evil perpetrations inflicted on God's chosen Pilot Project that involved the heritage of Abraham, Isaac, and Jacob in Medieval Europe.

There were four kinds of Jews who were vomited out of Spain and Portugal in those disgraceful days. (We won't even discuss the blood-stained Inquisitions of France and her European neighbors nearby!) But in the Spanish Inquisition of the Iberian Peninsula there were four groups:

- *Conversos,* who outwardly converted to the Roman Church scenario but were never really trusted by non-Jews of the community.

- *Crypto Jews,* who were forcibly pressured into a "conversion." Yet all the while they continued to practice their biblical Torah background in secret, though never without intense surveillance and fear of persecution.

- *Maranos*—the term for *pigs* in early Spanish—who refused baptism outright. They were also known as *anusim,* or "*unwilling,*" and as refugees, ran for their lives whenever and wherever they might.

- There were also on-the-spot *refuseniks,* who on their rejection to publicly submit to a forced baptism were forthwith burned at the stake or beheaded by the guillotine—all of this in God's Name!

Nor is it any wonder why there is such an array of God-rejection today, or on the other hand, why the Almighty has deferred justice for the victimized for so long! And now Islamists, with a similar spirit to compel submission, are once more waiting in the wings for yet another rerun of Act II repression!

But then there are also others of us who are confidently and prayerfully waiting for the Almighty's Act III for a Grand Finale! We need You, Abba!

A New Start in a New World

Therefore, late in time but timely enough, the door opening into a New World was a breath of fresh air. Unfortunately, there also grew airs of elitism, self-devised democratic dominance, and a tad of superiority over the slower plodders who failed to catch on to a new competitive world in a sort of economic Olympics. But for most aspects of justice and fairness, it was better than before and good for starters at least.

So guess where the Maranos, the Conversos—aka "new" Christians—and the Cryptos headed? And along with them not a few just ordinary Jews! That's not to mention all those other non-Jews who chose to actually worship God and not an intimidating "religious" system. Yes, it had benefits.

But before we flit across a new scenario to check out any Y chromosome of the future from Canada to Chile, just where did Captain Colombo hail from anyway?

I found an excellent report of an interview by Veteran Jewish historian Cecil Roth with Rabbi William Berkowitz, giving us some rare personal insights into the celebrated Super-Sailor.[2] Historian Roth gives us at least three clues on something that was indeed interesting if not unique to the exalted explorer.

On his correspondence, Christopher always made some unexplained tiny squiggles in the upper right hand corner of his letters, which turned out to be eventually deciphered as AAA, the Marano abbreviation for Adonai[3] for which any Hebrew speaker has no difficulty catching.

In a second scenario, everything seemed to be shipshape and ready to go, from tides to trade winds, for Columbus's initially scheduled departure date on August 2, 1492—all but Colombo the man, that is! The *Santa Maria*'s OIC seemed to be dawdling elsewhere! Maybe he couldn't find an ATM! Maybe not!

As it turned out, August 3rd of that year was the 9th of Av.[4] And any Hebrew watcher well knows that the 9th of Av is *not* the wisest day to check out on a maiden voyage for trans-Atlantic travel, then or even now!

Then in another leaked slip of the lip, at one point the courageous captain was heard discussing long-term chronology, mentioning the "lapse of 1400 years since the destruction of the Second House." Ironically, that was his cryptogram for the razing of the Second *Temple* by the Romans—of all people—in Jerusalem!

His choice of terminology didn't sound like credible Catholic culture-of-the-day conversation to Roth, nor does it to anyone else unless you're Jewish!

And one more Hebraic hint across the entirety of the historic "Spanish" hero's travel plans, was its makeup of a well represented number of "new Christians" (aka Conversos) in his several expeditions. They were chosen to be used as translators or even associate explorers for new opportunities in a new world. So was Christopher Jewish?

Go figure.

So Where Are They Now?

To unravel all the threads of destiny of the millions of Maranos, Conversos, Cryptos, anusim, and even the scattered myriad of otherwise religious or even secular Jews into the New World is an unquestionable foray into futility.

For my own curiosity, when I meet someone with a Latin American name like Sanchez, Hernandez, Gomez, Gonzales, Fernandez, or a variety of others, it is truly a valid conversation catcher for historical origins. I find it an invariably positive marker of Marano heritage for which I could see anyone might be justifiably pleased. And just as predictably, I find that most of these names have some sort of faith-orientation to which there ought to be no regret.

So, thanks, Colombo, for giving all these friends of ours a lift over in your day!

Checking the Jewish populations across Latin America, it is very hard to say what percentages of them might be former Conversos—it is reported most eventually returned to their Hebraic roots—including the Cryptos, or even the broader classification of Maranos.

Of the nearly half a million Jews in the Latin American rooted nations of Spain and Portugal, Argentina has the seemingly highest number of more than 200,000 Jews; and Brazil is second with an estimated 100,000.[5] Uruguay, Mexico, and Chile all follow with respectable Jewish communities of scattered Jewish identity, Crypto included. And there are many more across Central America, most certainly with a high ratio of Crypto, Conversos, and Maranos.

Sadly, to the chagrin of a shifting southwestern USA, whose comfort zones may inwardly struggle unwittingly with prophetic planning, Crypto migration is steadily moving into New Mexico and well across southern Texas.

Thus, if these present population moves are interpreted as mere political grabs for personal greed on either side of the Latino–US border—it has its problems. But what if a few millennia ago, the Almighty already had this bit of 2012 destiny on the back burner for His scheduled scattering of Father Abram's Y chromosome when He drew him out from Ur of the Chaldeans?[6] Does our comprehension of the Most High actually put Him high enough to realize that even way back in Ur, He would have known the very day, month, and year He planned to shift more of the Maranos across to Texas? For any and all who abhor mixing "religion with politics," the corollary of the concept is the mindless risk of mixing politics with Heaven's Annual Planner!

If the Ancient of Days is timeless, tense-less, and omniscient, it's time we looked at life in terms of Abba's own To-Do Today Diary! Come on, think! If God is God, when did He begin to initiate His planning for your day today?

So I presume I'll back off from offering my advice on this elusive border bumble. However, it will be interesting to watch if any thus far unknown "Genetically Modified" influences should shortly begin casting that long-awaited celestial canopy across an end-of-days renewal just waiting to surface! Perhaps some apt advice is to quit fussing and start fasting!

And that could well add the question of how many in the current people movement are from any ancient flow-on of Crypto Jews? No one except the Ancient of Days perhaps has the accurate stats. But as I was researching these data, I just received a late-line, stop-the-presses e-mail reply from a rabbinical contact in New Mexico who knows these folks that went like this:

> Thank you for writing.
>
> There have been many estimates done on the Crypto Jews of the Americas. These studies have been done by Jews in Yisrael. We have our own numbers from various studies which we have done. The majority of Hidden Jews are found in Brasil and Mexico, an estimated 10–15 million in Brasil and 5 million in Mexico. Other countries like Chile, the information is hard to come by. We are still compiling information.

Excuse me! An estimated 10–15 million Cryptos in Brazil, and 5 million in Mexico when the official numbers given for registered Jews in both countries are only 100,000 and 40,000 respectively? What's going on here? Yet the good rabbi works with these folks! And his website and physical address appear to be anything but flaky!

Moreover, we have been looking for potential possibilities, not countable birth certificates, since page one, so we're quite on course dealing with estimates!

So what does it matter anyway? When it comes to Abraham's genetically modified gene pool, all we know is it's mushrooming by the minute, and there's one and only one Sovereign Statistician who actually has the full story. So we'll probably have to wait in the queue for a while for our need to know!

So Does That Give the Story for All the Western Hemisphere?

Well, not exactly! I just got another e-mail from a colleague sensitive to my subject. The title was *Missouri Cherokee Tribes Proclaim Jewish Heritage.*[7] The article on its own may or may not be of sensational status. He claimed oral legends from the Cherokee of the Old Louisiana Purchase do have some interesting coordination with the *Sicarii* Zealots who fought the Romans as guerrillas at the time of the 72–73 CE Masada siege, i.e., *Sicarii* [see-car-ree] bearing so-so linguistic linkage to suggest a cognitive connection with "*Cherokee.*"

However, even though that in *itself* hardly harkens to history, what does matter is that it's *not* by itself. It's one of a lengthening queue of claims that North American Indian tribes go back to Babel or even closer to biblical names we might recognize.

The late Dr. Barry Fell in his book, *Saga America,*[8] documents a Hebrew-like inscription called The Bat Creek Stone, which was found in the American Southeast in the region of the Cherokee near the Tennessee-North Carolina border. The stone itself, which contains one mere line of dubious Paleo Hebrew, has raised a fury of controversy among the local lads of learning. However its credibility had also been defended and documented by both Drs. Fell and Gordon. Dr. Gordon's book *Before Columbus*[9] includes a scathing rebuke to those who attempt to deny the authenticity of the article, which he had dated to the second century CE, while Dr. Fell likewise documented Hebrew-language coins found in Kentucky, Missouri, and Arkansas.[10]

However, regardless of whether the tangible artifacts are hoax or Heaven-sent, what remained to be reckoned with was the abundance of Cherokee trails of truth that undeniably lead back to more recognizable roots of origin.

A letter from a Georgian of Cherokee ancestry in the 1986 ESOP[11] papers commented on a Cherokee legend that a race of pygmies once inhabited the Southern Appalachians. This Cherokee myth was laughed at by traditional establishment types until pygmy skeletons were actually found in the region. Evidence presented in Chapter 3 of Barry Fell's book, *Bronze Age America*,[12] confirmed that such a race *did* exist and their skulls are photographed for that book as evidence. Also noteworthy is that the Cherokee word for this pygmy race has the same root word as the languages of Old World languages, indicating either a Cherokee origin in the Old World or contact with Old World groups.[13]

Researchers into the pre-Columbus population of the New World find Barry Fell's trilogy of books[14] to be astounding. He deals mostly with North America, but his studies have uncovered mountains of evidence regarding the Indians on that continent. And he additionally traces the migration of the Micmac, Algonquin, Iroquois, Zuni, and Pima Indians in his research.

Thus, having noted a few of the former potential candidates for a Paleo Hebrew class, our next stop should perhaps be Hidden Mountain near Los Lunas, New Mexico!

Between a Rock and an Eye-Opener: The Decalogue Stone

We've looked at famous finds and disputed dates, mistreated minorities and unwanted worshippers in privately programmed parishes—center stage has been the hated and harangued Jew! But irony of ironies, we perceive a Genetic Designer who seems all the more determined to distribute their unwanted genetics to the ends of the earth—in fact, to a presumably untainted New World to those tricks of so-called Jewish treachery.

Amazing! Is it the Great Designer's unique craftsmanship that so makes these anti-Semites cringe, or is it that the Creator Himself thinks so diversely from a humanistic planet that He has to maintain His own charts for steering the ship?

These things you have done and I kept silent; you thought I was altogether like you. But I will rebuke you and accuse you to your face.[15]

But just when an age of Hellenistically hatched humanists begin to feel they had finally found freedom from a fictitious Heaven's hang-ups to lifestyles of license, lucre, and lust, some illiterate "savage" comes out of the bushes to discover the Decalogue Stone complete with the Bible's Top Ten "Thou Shalt Not's" in ancient Paleo Hebrew.

"It's gotta be a hoax" echo the experts from the civil liberties camp who are out to prohibit such church and state subversion in the USA. They've got proof: *"No one was here before Columbus and the 'savages'."* And this is the academic drivel of the educated elite! "Fourteen hundred and ninety-two, Columbus sailed the ocean blue." See, they've also done Grade One!

Ironically it appears that some of those earlier "savages" may well have been able to read Paleo Hebrew a bit more efficiently than the less-Hebraic politically correct counterfeits who would be more skilled at the janitorial jobs of removing Scripture proclamations from the halls of government!

Unbelievable!

But now let's have a good look at the Decalogue Stone ourselves in a classic report on "The Los Lunas Hebrew Inscription"[16] by Jeff A. Benner, founder of the Ancient Hebrew Research Center.

There is no point for me to overly repeat Benner's excellent article on the one-of-a-kind discovery. Anyone can download it. Well, it was one-of-a-kind in North America perhaps; but the irony is—as Benner tells us—it was almost identical to a Tel Dan inscription in northern Israel. I have personally visited the Tel Dan site myself. It had been dated to 1,000 BCE, and was crafted into the *identical* Paleo Hebrew script in New Mexico, which we are about to appreciate.

Moreover, another illuminating encounter with the remarkable rock was with the late Professor Frank Hibben (1910–2002), who was interviewed in 1996 by Professor James Tabor of the Department of Religious Studies from the University of North Carolina. Hibben, likewise a retired University of New Mexico archaeologist, attested that he first saw the incredible inscription of Los Lunas in 1933. The massive smooth rock face was lodged on Hidden Mountain at an angle of about 40 degrees clockwise from horizontal and had, over the centuries, edged about two-thirds of the way down from the summit. Hibben claims his mature-age guide told him at the time that he himself first saw the awesome stone tablet phenomenon as a young boy, sometime around the 1880s.

And a third extraordinary corroborative report of the genuineness of the text was from the Qumran Cave 1 (I've also visited that specific area a few times). Comparing the ancient Tetragrammation (Hebrew: *yod-hey-vav-hey*) of the 100 BCE Habakkuk commentary from Qumran, with the three appearances of YAHWEH on the Decalogue Stone in Los Lunas, again vouches for the amazing authenticity of the North American inscriptions.

As a professional linguist, the Decalogue Stone lettering, the irregularities, the reports, and the explanations, together with the odd inclusions of a few select Greek letters, as well as the manner of professional interpretation, all make good sense. What the various reports that I have studied do *not* prove are the exact dates of the inscriptions, the identity of the authors, or the circumstances involving their authorship, their particulars of contact, or even their purpose.

What they do confirm is a heavy involvement of the Tribe of Dan, possible involvement of the now nearly extinct tribe of Samaritans, and what is proven with certainty is post-Sinai, post-Mosaic involvement of Israelites linked with the Abrahamic Y chromosome. And consequently, that justifies including these few pages into this text.

I personally find the research most fascinating, and not the least amusing considering that the Ancient of Days chose to plant that staggering Decalogue Stone on state-owned turf! So cry your hearts out, all politically correct pagans who elect to upstage the Almighty. I'd like to watch when you try to remove that some ninety ton Monument to Ten Counts of Morality—or is it immorality?—off of state-owned Hidden Mountain!

There is so much to probe about this unique phenomenon engineered by El Shaddai Himself, so I do urge you to do yourself a favor to research it all. You can learn an abundance more by Googling "*The New Mexico Decalogue Stone*" in general, and as noted above, downloading "The Los Lunas Inscription" by Jeff A. Benner in particular. It's a worthwhile effort.

Brazil's Grassroots Debut to a New Day

Finally one passing, but ever so fond farewell to Brazil, as we file away Abraham's Y chromosome in the Western Hemisphere! And I do not believe in coincidences! Luck—good luck or bad luck! *Luck* is a four-letter fraud in my dictionary, and there can be *nothing* that "just happens." The universe in its entirety is from the divine Diary of the Ancient of Days. If Abba is Abba, it is impossible for me—or you—to comprehend otherwise.

As I was putting together this chapter in the ancient pulse of those "*stars of the sky and the sands of the sea*" promises to Abraham, I got one more very brief e-mail midway in the editing from a cherished colleague—the interim executive director of the International Christian Embassy in Jerusalem. The ICEJ is a service organization for a new generation of Christian believers to bless their Jewish counterparts in Israel. What light there had been in the Dark Ages has long sputtered out. Today the lights are flickering on for a new generation of enlightened Judeo-Christian relationships. It's wholly from the heart and hardly from any physical headquarters!

Of all days, times, or seasons for this report to come regarding Brazil, no lottery of luck, no finger of fate, and no proverbial rocket scientist could have hit it more precisely.

What is happening in Brazil in this very week of my writing is what also began among the Waolas in Papua New Guinea in my early 1961 contact with that little clutch of Stone Age searchers in the simplest of scenarios.[17] What happened on that precise morning in an unsolicited moment of truth to a rainforest tribe of Third World status has since, tribe by tribe, washed across their entire island nation. It had flashed a preview of exactly what is now also beginning in these days in a Third World Brazil. Someone somewhere must be flipping on the lights one by one!

But even for its land mass, an immense Third World Brazil plus a substantial California-sized Third World Papua New Guinea are but two tiny microbe-like specks on an infinite sphere of 6 billion souls. So either you see that Hand writing in the halls of Heaven or you don't—either there is light—real light, or there is darkness. That's all!

Here's a paraphrase of my colleague's brief Brazilian report noted:

I am writing this prayer update from Manaus overlooking the Rio Negro in the Amazon rainforest of Brazil. Manaus, a city of 2 million inhabitants, is today one of the most God-oriented cities in the world: more than half the population are dedicated Bible believers! On days of worship the public transport system needs to be run at 100 percent capacity as the streets are packed with people headed for prayer.

The congregation of Pastor Rene Terra Nova started less than twenty years ago in a small garage in a suburb of Manaus. Today they have some 70,000 followers. When the overflowing fellowship decided to build their first large sanctuary, they began by building a prayer tower, which to this day is used twenty-four hours a day to pray for their city, their country, and, may we never forget, the nation of Israel. Prayer is considered a primary key for today's revival in South America.

We will touch on the phenomenon again in the end of these Genetically Modified insights. There is both the natural Seed of Abraham and the Genetically Modified Seed of Abraham—together looking for an Abba. Or in technical language, is it a Y chromosome biologically searching to connect to its Designer? Or is it an Olive Tree looking for Eden's original Gardener?

Hang in there! The Western world is unraveling, but this may be just exactly what we've been waiting for in that colossal climax!

CHAPTER 11

Lost Tribes Fever

In 2 Kings 17:5–6, we have the biblical account of King Shalmaneser of Nineveh attacking Israel (what else is new?) in something like 722 BCE and hauling ten of Israel's tribes off to Assyria. The story goes like this:

> *The king of Assyria invaded the entire land, marched against Samaria and laid siege to it for three years. In the ninth year of Hoshea, the king of Assyria captured Samaria and deported the Israelites to Assyria. He settled them in Halah, in Gozan on the Habor River and in the towns of the Medes.*

Enter: The Lost Tribes! Or should we say "exit"?

Now the physical transfer of the tribes of Israel is an historical reality borne out particularly by the biblical account, as well as secular historical records and a multitude of both ancient and modern books from Josephus to E. Raymond Capt. Capt has been previously cited in Chapter 3, brilliantly detailing much of the earlier relocation of those exiled Israelites, albeit I do have a problem or two with his eventual conclusions as to where they all eventually ended up in later movements. Nevertheless, credit where credit is due!

However, like any dire disaster, some of the flow-on interpretation will be true and some of it will not be true. Take 9-11. There are those who say with predictable vitriol that it must be the Jews who did it; others have "proof beyond a shadow of doubt" that it was an inside job by the American government themselves. Then of course, it was the Muslims, though the *M* word in some circles has been declared politically incorrect for obvious cover-up, even though the four pilots and their fifteen militant mates who perished with the plot were actually mentored a tad closer to Mecca than to Mars! Other opinions are all of the above, none of the above, or other incidental insights. But you get the picture of agenda-oriented reporting.

Thus we may get a similar array of interpretations with the whereabouts of the aftermath of the Lost Tribes. The point is, there was indeed an event, but after that, a certain amount of speculation moves in, some of which can be believed and some which cannot. Unfortunately there are always those knee-jerk naysayers who are inclined to jettison Junior with the bathwater. Fortunately there is an abundance of Bible to follow on after 2 Kings 17:5–6 if anyone cares to read it. Indeed, interpretations abound, but if one follows the "two or three principle" of multi-text witnesses, that's a reasonably safe position to take.

So this might be the time for me to restate—if it's not abundantly clear already from the above paragraph—it's hardly the data itself that sours the senses of any or all of those who search out a new—or old— happening. Unfortunately the agenda of many "armchair analysts" may give us their private take on what it means to them, which can lead to error on *either* side of the data. Lost Tribes fever, spiritual renewal movements, and not the least, treasured theological tenets of well-pickled tradition, are all subject to private preconceptions. Be careful— two or three witnesses please!

Thus, I would like to clearly reiterate that my primary channel for writing this book is not to make nationalistic mileage into which nation some of these scattered souls may have surfaced, but rather to keep a focus on the enormity of the "stars of the sky and the sands of the sea" metaphor. So for this reason, I have purposely bypassed some of the more prominently researched refugees, and tried to pick up on the less likely carriers of the clandestine Y chromosome of the forefathers.

Moreover, we will eventually touch on a few of those better known historical anecdotes yet in this chapter. But my main point is that those lost legends with the most previous publicity may be a pittance compared to others we had not yet considered—like the improbable genetic potential in the Orient or the South Pacific Islands where we began.

And as we have already run into a few more newcomers to what we might call a "Crypto-fest," there will have even been a multitude of yet other movements of the Most High's scatterings. There have been and will be select sand and star symbolisms that most of us had scarcely supposed.

That end-of-days revelation of all the ultimate extended family is apt to be BIG, BIG, BIG! Could we name it "Abba's Last Call to Dinner," or in the culture I grew up in, "Suppertime"?

And DNA might randomly be an alternative acronym for "Do Not Assume." Do not assume that the Almighty will let those promises to Abraham, the parallel inheritances for Isaac, and the immeasurable blueprint for an ingathered Israel of eternal dimensions all go up in a puff of blue smoke! Following the current final flash of humanistic rebellion and blasphemous challenge, one could certainly question whether He is about to jettison the supremacy of His creation to the dustbin of history. I am sure the hour is coming when the Ancient of Days will have had enough.

Enter: Sand, Stars, and divine Sovereignty—including a word of encouragement from Isaiah 29:5–8:

> *But your many enemies will become like fine dust, the ruthless hordes like blown chaff. Suddenly, in an instant, the LORD Almighty will come with thunder and earthquake and great noise, with windstorm and tempest and flames of a devouring fire. Then the hordes of all the nations that fight against Ariel [aka Jerusalem], that attack her and her fortress and besiege her, will be as it is with a dream, with a vision in the night—as when a*

hungry man dreams that he is eating, but he awakens, and his hunger remains; as when a thirsty man dreams that he is drinking, but he awakens faint, with his thirst unquenched. So will it be with the hordes of all the nations that fight against Mount Zion.

A Blog from the *Jerusalem Post* on the Matter

One of a multitude[1] of Zionist-oriented Bible enthusiasts has been published a few times in the *Jerusalem Post*, including an interesting blog on some of the very things we have been considering. In October 2010, he published a most interesting title: "Zionist Christians might be from Israel's 'Ten Lost tribes'." Here is his opening segment:

We are witnessing an amazing turn of events in Jewish/Christian history. After nearly two millennia of animosity and distrust, we see large numbers of Christians loving Jews. And Jews worldwide are responding and appreciating Christians for their friendship and strong support of Israel. Perhaps no greater evidence of this new congeniality is the very magazine you are holding: a special monthly edition of *The Jerusalem Post* dedicated to Christian lovers of Zion.

This new mutual warmth has caused many Jews and Christians to remark that we have more in common with each other—in spite of our different beliefs regarding Jesus—than we do with many of our coreligionists. For we are as far removed from our Jimmy Carters and Reverend Jeremiah Wrights as the Jewish Zionists are from their Noam Chomskys and Richard Goldstones.

The swiftness of the change has also caused many within the Christian *Zionist movement* to wonder if there isn't more going on here. Is our sudden passionate defense of Israel being driven by something deeper than just our common biblical heritage? Could we actually be witnessing the fulfillment of the most prophesied event in the Bible—the reunion of the House of Israel with the House of Judah? More to the point, could we Christians be actual descendants of the missing Ten Tribes of the House of Israel, captured by Assyria and scattered among the nations in 722 BCE? More and more Christians (myself included), and even some Jews, have come to this startling conclusion!

Although the event is foretold by all of Israel's prophets, none described it more graphically than Ezekiel. Given a vision of a valley covered with dry bones, he was asked by an angel, "Son of man, can these bones live?" When he could not answer, the angel told him to command the breath [Holy Spirit] to breathe "on these slain that they may come to life." So he did, "and they came to life and stood on their feet, an exceedingly great army." He was then informed: "Son of man these bones are the whole house of Israel" (see Ezekiel 37:1–14).

The bottom line is that more than 80 percent of Jacob's family is still missing and have had 2,700 years to intermarry with every nationality. Today they probably number in the hundreds of millions. Where are they? How will we know them? And if we are in the Last Days, as most of us believe, how will they be found in time to be reunited with Judah?

The author adds considerably more discussion in his treatise, which we will not include here, and concludes his *JPost* article with these final paragraphs:

We also have John's description of the heavenly city of Jerusalem in the book of Revelation having only 12 gates, each named after one of the 12 tribes of Israel (see Revelation 21:12). There is no gate marked "Christian." Or any back door for "righteous gentiles."

. . . many readers are no doubt thinking, "If this is true, how would so many Christians ever fit into Israel?" Although not all will come home, for only "a remnant will be saved" (Isaiah 10:22; Romans 9:27), still the number would be quite large. That makes this prophecy by Isaiah all the more intriguing: *"The children of whom you were bereaved will yet say in your ears, 'The place is too cramped for me; make room for me that I may live here.' Then you will say in your heart; Who has begotten these for me. . . . Behold I was left alone, from where did these come?"* (Isaiah 49:20, 21)

I guess the Lord Himself will eventually make it clear whether we Christian Zionists are the missing tribes. A recent news item even suggests a possible way. A new genetic study has shown that worldwide Jewry all share the same genome, proving they constitute "one family." Maybe it's time we non-Jewish lovers of Israel take the same test.

Interesting!

Though the *Post* published this article almost ten months ago, I had it on file but confess I hadn't really read it thoroughly until now. Why? Because it is hardly new to a multitude of Christian Zionists. What is new, however, is that it was published in the *Jerusalem Post* with a bit more Christian content than they might ordinarily print, and unwittingly to me, at the moment it fits hand in glove to the genetic "modification" of Abraham's Y chromosome scattered worldwide as I have been presenting thus far.

Moreover, also new is the timing of my pulling the article out of my last year's files, and the irony that I *must* include it in this very chapter as I touch on my personal history, and the cultural Bible Belt cradle into which I was birthed.

The Psychoanalysis of a Wannabe

I once heard a less than Jew-loving lecturer mocking the "Wannabes"—those simpleminded souls who, on hearing about the heritage of the Hebrews since Sunday school happenings, would somehow like to be one of them. But can a leopard change its spots?[2]

Possibly he doesn't have to! What if the Wannabe actually is one?

Now I won't deny for one moment that every society has a few loose bricks in every load of building blocks! We'll always have those insecure entities that have to be different to prove the point of their presence. I mean some fads do produce fanatics, but in my several decades of waking up to the reality of Hebraic roots, I've met thousands of people, but I can count on one hand the loonies that started to run around Goyim Central Mall with prayer shawls and *kippot*.

But from what we have discovered so far, if Abraham's Y chromosome is as prevalent as presented, it will come as no surprise that a few of us wouldn't be picking up a tad of our attachment to ancient ties.

Interesting biblical linkages that I hadn't yet noted are the four overall mentions of God's discipline to "those that hate me to the third and fourth generation."[3]

And an add-on to that are five repeats of promises of blessing *"to a thousand generations of those who love Me and keep My commandments!"*[4]

The irony is—and I choose my terms carefully—that religious kneejerk, Jew or Gentile, is sometimes a bit hard to pin down in the Holy Writ. But when you get down to the fine print, the name of the game is always *obedience*. And that's what either links up or else breaks links with the Most High to those three, four, or one thousand follow-on generations. Anyone ready for a nice new Y chromosome for the next 1,000 years? But it could cost you a bit of independence, aka freedom, as some would value it!

"But that's Old Testament stuff" comes as an echo! May I remind you that so are the Ten Commandments, Genesis, Exodus, the Psalms, Isaiah 9, 53, and a few other bits of behavior!

If anyone is feeling a bit short-changed at the moment from the not-too-deep wading pools of western pop theology, there is hope.

The Scriptures also declare—twice—that a Moabite, an Arabic descendant of Lot, may not enter the congregation—aka the Hebraic family—for ten generations.[5] That's a while to wait for your passport!

But if you study the story of Ruth (the Moabitess), she walked right in! Not only did she sail on through, she even fell into the lineage of the Messiah. It's all on who you know—that's for sure! And who you know is *not* religion. It's relationship.

"And your people shall be my people and your God my God."[6]

Any anti-Semites out there still listening?

Anabaptist Bonuses

Let's get back to where I started to tell you about my "tad of attachment to ancient ties." I grew up in the "Bible Belt"[7] of Midwest America. My early orientation was a mixture of general Brethrenish worldview and Anabaptist behavior.

Everything from my Sunday school teachers to Scripture memory taught me to never jettison the Jews—God's Chosen People! Actually I never knew any—so I presumed. And that's why my Israeli friends today—close friends, I might say—tell me, "That's why you liked the Jews—you didn't know any!"

But today, some seventy years on through my realm of reason, I've learned a few things. Possibly one is that whole Bible Belt from Pennsylvania to El Paso might even be a bit Jewish—I did say *might*!

Be careful also—I didn't say *kosher* and I didn't say *Halakkic*[8]—I said Jewish—Hebraic heritage. That BB stretch of culture wouldn't have known a Y chromosome from a Model T Ford, but after decades of recent reflection, many of us are wondering if a bit of Abraham's issue was more than present. But we never knew it!

By the time I was forty—possibly even before—I began to think more seriously about my ancestry. The early family never discussed it much, and today we certainly see why. It was dangerous in Europe from Constantine on, and Connie's ghost seems to be back for an encore!

One thing I did learn about my Hungarian grandfather (a "Magyar" to those in the area) was what my widowed mother on occasion told us—her "Pop" was always "good with the Jews." Forty more years on, I'm sure he was one!

The mindless who mock the Wannabes understand neither the depth of the human psyche nor the pigeons that pervert our patio. No matter how many times you drive them off, homing pigeons always find their way back! My childhood culture shouts a little louder—especially from some of that strange stuff from the homespun church in the countryside, compared to the towering cathedrals in the cities. Sixty-five years on, it doesn't seem strange at all in Jerusalem!

But my long journey of yesteryear actually proves nothing unless nostalgia is data for the debate. The men sat on one side and the ladies on the other—a bit of a letdown for lusty-eyed young lads! But these days I've discovered some ancient trends that did it the same way—from Jerusalem to Papua New Guinea I might add. The service of bygone years always began with an Old Testament reading followed by a New Testament text. It wasn't exactly a teaching of Torah, but neither did it minimize Moses.

An Orthodox rabbi friend of ours in Jerusalem, who occasionally teaches a class to some of his Christian Zionist admirers, once commented that he can never comprehend those Christians who put their Bibles on the floor. Nothing new here, either! When I was a kid, my mother laid it on the line whenever anyone in the family laid the Holy Writ on the woodwork. And another Hebraism, for all newborn lads circumcision was a given.

And then the ladies' head coverings also abounded. (Not to be confused with the Islamic *burka*, whose source and purpose is a paradigm shift from the rest of civilization.) Today much of this has long been westernized across the Bible Belt. But in the early days, Moses was anything but a mystery.

Back in European roots they met only in homes within walking distance of the congregation. The leader wore no elaborate robes but opened the Good Book in impromptu fashion and taught the people. Those were the roots!

From the beginning Rome detested the Jew as a challenger to her prowess of power. But the irony was that the offspring of Abraham were never alone then, nor are they now. There were the Waldensians who, along with the Jews, were an early target of the Church. For two or three centuries at least, the Waldensians continued to keep Shabbat. And what had also been called "The Church in the Wilderness" was reported to have had roots from the first-century era, frequently bypassing Rome entirely.

They would also have been Sabbath keepers from the beginning, as was early Christianity in Spain. But all of these non-conformists to the Roman hierarchy found themselves quite in the queue to face the guillotine or be burned at the stake right along with the Jews. And all of these movements were without question much closer to Jerusalem than a notoriously anti-Semitic Roman Church.

Nazarene, Hebraic, the Wilderness, or who knows? All were in the cookie cutter for the Bible Belt and today bear the phenomena of a hunger for our erstwhile Hebraic heritage. All were melded together against the attacks of Rome and most have reflected potential patrimony of the Patriarchs.

Abraham's Y chromosome again seemingly penetrated the Bible Belt but on quite another train than the Maranos. That's my point—a Y chromosome is a Y chromosome! And at the final trumpet, not even the Most High can moot the difference.

But that's only a pittance of my own journey to Jerusalem. My origins were minute indeed.

We must add to that the much wider array of Anabaptist roots, the not insignificant Mennonite distribution across the western world in general and the Bible Belt in particular. In November 2010 there was the heretofore unheard of visit—from buggy to Airbus—of an Amish delegation of forty-five of the faithful to Jerusalem to render an apology to Israel for past rejection and a future pledge of support in any way possible.[9]

At this point I dare not pass up the opportunity to report on the bulls-eye linguistics, innocently coined by an Ohio pastor who came with me on an earlier tour in 1997. The good pastor without an iota of ill-will whatsoever, in his first encounter with the Ultra Orthodox of Jerusalem, distinguished them as "the Amish Jews."

Look, if you've never lived any portion of your lives in Amish country, you've missed a good deal of your education!

But moving on to the Mennonites, they were far more numerous in my high school years than were the Amish, as they are, as well, from Switzerland across North America. I have friend after Mennonite friend who has acknowledged to me that they too were unquestionably of Jewish heritage.

Perhaps the most significant contact, however, was a visit to world-famous Behalt Mennonite Heritage Center[10] in Millersburg, Ohio, that features the 265-foot circular mural of Anabaptist history. The director of the center at the time confirmed to me that most certainly, a very high percentage of Mennonites were also of mixed Jewish heritage—always room for a few more million Y chromosomes it would seem!

Thus the scope of a bizarre family, stitched together with bits and pieces of humanity, ever spreads with an unprecedented promise of Hebraic potential!

Let Us Lastly Consider the Controversial Khazar

Some years ago I read an intriguing book by veteran author Arthur Koestler, which he called *The Thirteenth Tribe*.[11]

Back in the seventh century CE, there was a Central Asian people—said to be Turkic by some—dwelling between the Black Sea on the west and the Caspian Sea to the east just under the shadow of the lofty Caucasus Mountains on the north.

They were known as Khazars and their land was Khazaria. For your future information to speculate where they may have headed when their super-state collapsed around 900 CE: Bulgaria was located a bit to the south, the Slavic states were much to the west, the Magyars—my grandfather's clan—were a nudge to the northwest, and Kiev was a bit beyond that. And Russia was even farther north. These were all within walking distance from Khazaria, of course! Well, I should say, within walking distance if your country caves in when you least expected it! And then as any cartographer can clarify, Western Europe is just a tad beyond Slavic Eastern Europe, and that also is exactly where a majority of the Jew-loving Bible Belters came from!

According to Koestler, these Khazars had a problem but with no particular precedent of a realistic solution to pursue. The Arabs—aka emerging militant Muslims—were spoiling their scenery to the east and the Byzantine era Greek Orthodox of Constantinople caliber was uncomfortably close on the west—and getting closer!

Their leader was known as a Khagan Zechariah (read: Headhoncho Zechariah). And he got a bright idea. He had heard of some impressive folks down in Samaria—that's where the Lost Tribes got lost from, if you recall? So he sent down to the former Ten Tribes territory to hire a priest to come up to Khazaria and teach them how to become Jews. Unfortunately it was a bit of political posturing to keep the neighbors east and west in check, but fortunately if the King of the Universe has a Plan, He's been known to use the short-sightedness of the secular in His own game. And so it was!

Before we finish the tale, let me ask you: Was this headman Khagan Zechariah fellow Jewish? You might just as well get your guess in now, before you get the full facts, because all the people who have probed the problem and their ideas on it, already have twenty different opinions to give us. So make a guess from what you already perceive of from human behavior! What do you reckon?

Indeed, the Khazars became a strong political entity lodged between the Muslim east and the Greek Orthodox west. In fact, they became the superpower of the Khazaria area, stretching over two centuries from between 650–850 CE. They were superior, they were successful, and they were impressive in strategy. Let me ask again: Do you think head man Zechariah, or even many of the Khazars themselves, had any of that Y chromosome we've been thinking about? What did Zechariah know about priests vis-à-vis witch doctors, sorcerers, or shaman? Just wondered, that's all!

Were they merely recycled Turks, as some of the less ingenious may argue, or were they a bit of that Samaritan remnant that were carted off to Assyria? Nineveh, ironically, is on a straight line south toward that former turf of those ten routed tribes of Israel.

I certainly can't prove it, but it seems that neither can any of the other assorted agendas of who the Khazars were and why.

For starters, the anti-Semites of Europe are certain that this cache of so-called Asians have no place whatsoever in Europe pretending to be Ashkenazi Jews. Nor would they be given the time of day anywhere among Europe's Jew-haters for that matter, reflecting any remnant of Adolf Shicklegruber's final solution. (If you don't remember who Shicklegruber is, try Google!)

And of course, the Muslim Brotherhood and friends likewise presume that if the Ashkenazi of Europe are now parading as Jews in Jerusalem, they need to be dealt with ever so starkly. The Iranian gestures of genocide will have no pity either upon even Central Asians who lust after Jerusalem.

And the so-called Palestinians would have similar solutions to "*prey for a piece of Jerusalem!*" No way could they recognize Khazars as Jews, and for that matter, neither Jews nor central Asians would be welcome to profane their presumed "Palestinian" turf from at least "5,000 years" duration, which happens to predate Adam by merely a millennia or so! Let's never let facts get mixed up with a good land grab, especially when your past or present neighbors—aka the Arab League—hint that they don't trust you, either!

But then we also have the other more positive people who can "prove" that the Khazars were truly Jews but who had actually moved on to London, Liverpool, or Lincoln, Nebraska, in a recycle of Israel's orbit. That's a little more humane but somehow I have a tad of trouble getting my head around that theory, either, especially when I read the prophets like Amos 9:15:

> "*I will plant Israel in their own land, never again to be uprooted from the land I have given them,*" says the LORD your God.

Or Jeremiah 23:8:

. . . but they will say, "As surely as the LORD lives, who brought the descendants of Israel up out of the land of the north (aka idolatry) and out of all the countries where he had banished them." Then they will live in their own land.

And Ezekiel 36:24:

"For I will take you out of the nations; I will gather you from all the countries and bring you back into your own land."

Or a multiple more like: Joel 3:20:

Judah will be inhabited forever and Jerusalem through all generations.

Somehow when the prophets of the Most High said New Jerusalem, I doubt they meant New Jersey, and when the Sovereign of the Galaxies says, "Never again," I have a little problem presuming He really meant "not again soon"!

Let's see in the next chapter if they're ready for us yet back in Israel.

CHAPTER 12

Seven Thousand More Headed Home

This book has had a buildup of added information sources like no other I have ever written. From the beginning, we have had clear-cut starting blocks with the indelible promises first to Abraham, and then to Isaac, and to Jacob after him. And we've had a clear-cut finish line to where we were headed from sandy seashores to a celestial countdown in the galaxies.

But the irony this time around is the closer we get to the finish line, the more information keeps pouring in. Possibly we could slow down a tad on new galaxy creations, Abba? It's getting harder for me to keep up!

What I've said from the beginning, however, was that we're not headed for every last corner that might detect a few Abrahamic chromosomes. But may we catch some of those less likely featured in an end-of-days finale for that fascinating collage of the Father's far-flung enormity of His promised family.

Within the last month, Arutz Sheva, the Jewish International News voice of Israel, headlined: *Israeli Government Allows 7000 Bnei Menashe to Make Aliyah*, that is, to come home to Israel. Perhaps this is just a testimony that the book is all the more timely to the magnitude of the moment.

Bnei Menashe actually means the "children of Manasseh," the

younger son of Joseph, Jacob's favorite lad whom his jealous brothers sold off into Egypt. But to truncate a very long tale, in June 2011, Israel's government gave an all-clear for this same Manasseh's descendants of twenty-nine centuries to finally head back home to their Promised Land!

Where Have the Bnei Menashe Been Hidden All This Time?

So like the Ethiopians in Chapter 9, the sons of Menashe are coming home at last, but where have they been hunkered down for over two millennia?

There's not too much conclusive to be said of their trail to Northeast India in those earliest days after their uprooting by Assyrian King Shalmanezer. The irony with the Tribe of Manasseh was that it had been divided into half. Half of them were allotted their portion of Canaan in the mountainous area of Samaria west of the Jordan River, while the other half were given their inheritance on the Golan Heights east of the Jordan.

Since this segment of Menashe had found its way down through central Asia to the southeast, it may be possible to presume that they had been the half living on the Golan and were driven on—or even by themselves had chosen—an escape route toward the south and east. The Silk Road—which we noted before in the case of Japanese context, or even possibly used earlier by the Karens of Myanmar—may also have been a factor?

An alternate route suggested in reports by Dr. Stephen Epstein, who did a serious study in detecting some of these devious detours, reports that they may have eventually fled Assyria via a Media-Persian route and from thence on through Afghanistan. From there they could have made their way to Hindu-Kush, traveling through Tibet and the Chinese city of Kaifeng.

Other oral traditions indicated that they had suffered considerable persecution and perhaps even slavery again in China, where initial segments of their fellow migrants supposedly splintered into alternate directions—some heading down the Mekong River into Vietnam, others to Thailand (formerly Siam), and still others venturing even farther southward by sea to the Philippines. From the oral recollections, others moved on into Burma (now Myanmar), and finally farther west into the Manipur and Mizoram Provinces of India, the present points for their departure home to Israel.[1]

One Bnei Menashe song, which had been handed down and carried throughout their travels, tellingly describes part of the Exodus from Egypt:

> *We must keep the Passover Festival*
> *Because we crossed the Red Sea on the dry land*
> *At night we crossed with a fire*
> *And by day with a cloud*
> *Enemies pursued us with chariots*
> *And the sea swallowed them up*
> *And used them as food for the fish*
> *And when we were thirsty*
> *We received water from the rock.*[2]

Epstein's report goes on to say:

> In 1951, a Pentecostal minister named Tchalah received a prophecy from God. He was told that his people must return to their original land and the faith they came from, *before* the war of Armageddon.[3]

Six decades on, they are finally forging through!

And Epstein then concludes his account of the Bnei Menashe with a touching cry for reuniting with "their brother Judah," i.e., today's Jewish community in modern Israel. He summarizes:

> The Bnei Menashe look to Zion, not for washing machines or microwaves, but for a fulfillment of a dream they carried with them during their exile of 2,700 years. A stanza of a modern poem they wrote speaks volumes:

Oh, my brother Judah
Unsatisfied with me,
Won't thou forgive me still, I pray;
Yet I don't think time is a barrier;
when the day of promise arrives. . . .[4]

It is only conjecture, but the western half of Manasseh may well have gone north toward greater Mesopotamia and were scattered, as well, with the nine-and-a-half remaining tribes of Jacob. But for the forebears of the 7,000 Bnei Menashe in question, they would have eventually made it as far as India's northeastern states of Manipur and Mizoram on the border with Myanmar on the east.

For these wandering exiles who finally faltered into India, the choice of temporary tenancy for a millennium or so might well have gone much worse. On the other hand, India wasn't the Golan, nor was it the ground deeded to Abraham and heirs. So it wasn't really home! But now it is, or soon will be!

And just for the record—in case Syrian President (aka dictator) Bashar al-Assad might have forgotten—half of that Lost Tribe of Manasseh, for some 700 years, had actually once inhabited what is known as the Golan Heights in today's terminology.

It is ironic that at the identical point in time that the Israeli government finally gave the Bnei Menashe the all-clear, the 2011 Syrian insurrection hit Bashar Assad like a time bomb. This is bizarre, because any collusion between the Israeli Department of the Interior or the Syrian rebels would have been off the planet—then, now, or even in the century to come—but it happened anyway! Someone above us earthlings would have certainly had His hand in it, so we'll have to wait to see how it plays out!

Anyway, Bashar Assad had previously been making a moderate fuss about Israel "giving him back" the Golan, which turf Israel had justifiably relieved Syria of in an otherwise unanticipated Middle East backlash back in 1967.

So how did Syria get mixed up in all this? Well, it so happened that the French of all people had been "gifted" with the Golan along with Arab Syria around 1920 by the thoughtful "generosity" of the League of Nations. Syria hung on to it until what appeared to be a bit of divine adjudication in that 1967 tangle with Israel. And Syria lost!

So to be fair, I looked this all up in the book of Joshua, and I could find no mention of the French, Syria, or the UN whatsoever—only God and this notable Israelite general named Joshua. So I'm satisfied that the Bnei Menashe can safely go ahead to make Aliyah! Aliyah, by the way, means "up" in Hebrew, and making Aliyah is an epithet for "going up"—that is, up to Jerusalem, the pinnacle of prominence in Abraham's promised inheritance.

It's hard to say if this 7,000 will actually go back to the Golan again since they're probably not the cattle ranchers they used to be under the watch of Moses. But regardless, they perhaps ought to go via Jerusalem anyway if for no other reason than to stop by and thank Shavei Israel Chairman Michael Freund for all his hard work since 2003 to make this high point happen!

Shavei Israel (formerly called Amishav) is the elite "Search and Rescue" operation organized to bring all these scattered souls home, and from the remainder of the sand and stars still out there, much effort still remains!

Twenty Million More Mushrooms

Seven thousand is no small success story, but on the other hand, as we mull over this milestone, it takes me back to our previous chapter of the "official" Jewish population listings for Latin America, in that all told, there were some 500,000 Jews in South and Central America. Then some rabbi in the know turns around and tells me that he works with these people and can estimate that there are 20 million more Cryptos in Brazil and Mexico alone! If you recall, Cryptos were the pseudonym of Jews who were forced into baptism by Rome, but who these days are coming back to their Hebraic roots in droves. Now that goes back a fair while ago, but the Creator is no amateur. Normal genetics are His biological fingerprints chiseled in stone!

Sorry for overplaying my Joe Stalin gem from Chapter 7 and most probably from others of my previous books in quoting what the Bolshevik Boss said about voting: "It doesn't matter who votes, but who counts the votes!" It's of course a fantastic insight into perverted politicians. But it's also a useful corollary—as crooked as its source has been—in genetically searching for stray souls. When all is said and done, dare I say: "It's not the one who does the DNA lab work, but the one who tallies up the data." If I read my Bible right, Abba does!

It may come as a surprise to some that God didn't invent democracy—the Greeks did! And if you happen to be the Creator you would have a bit of leeway the "created creature" doesn't have. For example, there are times like when Jeremiah visited the Potter's House in Jeremiah 18:1–10:

> *This is the word that came to Jeremiah from the LORD: "Go down to the potter's house, and there I will give you my message." So I went down to the potter's house, and I saw him working at the wheel. But the pot he was shaping from the clay was marred in his hands; so the potter formed it into another pot, shaping it as seemed best to him. Then the word of the LORD came to me: "O house of Israel, can I not do with you as this potter does?" declares the LORD. "Like clay in the hand of the potter, so are you in my hand, O house of Israel. If at any time I announce that a nation or kingdom is to be uprooted, torn down and destroyed, and if that nation I warned repents of its evil, then I will relent and not inflict on it the disaster I had planned. And if at another time I announce that a nation or kingdom is to be built up and planted, and if it does evil in my sight and does not obey me, then I will reconsider the good I had intended to do for it."*

So it looks like we're headed for a finale of divine DNA testing. If scattering one select servant's Y chromosome across climes, cultures, and eons gives the option of 20 million more "modified mushrooms"—aka chosen—to spring up overnight to tune in onto the Father's wavelength, that's well within tried-and-true technology from here to Houston! And without a doubt, it's from divine design most certainly even a tad higher than Houston!

And the good news is, if that family feature of the Y chromosome somehow never yet reached your village, the Master Potter has ways and means to reshape His clay for that, as well. All the bases were covered long ago!

Nor are we talking about alternate roads of atonement in that "all roads somehow lead to Rome." Not so! A more-than-prominent Prophet once declared of His own divine assignment, "It is finished," and so it was!

But this genetics thing that we have been looking at from page one onward is rather both *sensing and responding* to that "Last Call from Home." *Hearing* and *heeding* are opposite sides of the same coin. Once more I must refer to my Chapter 5 encounter with a dozen Stone Age total strangers to traditional theology. How could they begin to *know* a name for the King of Creation, for which half the Church and a significant segment of the synagogues don't have a clue?

Nor can top-drawer geneticists comprehend how anyone from rocket scientists to cave dwellers can pick up a signal from outer space to make friends with Abraham and family.[5] Let me tell you, it can be done and it is done routinely, and that's what Genetically Modified Promises are all about!

Looking Back—Looking Forward

So far throughout the book, we've been peeking around the far-flung perimeter of the Most High's worldwide genetic Masterpiece. An obvious awareness is that the present potential of the Family of Promise casts a very wide aura indeed. An omnipresent Father we cannot see, but His somewhat omnipresent family we may shortly be able to hazily make out as a few more end-of-an-era events begin to fall into place. Can we anticipate a global revival beginning with the Third World? The Hebrew word would be *shuv, "to return,"* that is—return to the Father!

But next a question: If there is a perimeter, must there be a center point, or is that irrelevant? Hardly! The Bible does indeed point to Jerusalem as a coming Center Stage—a New Jerusalem—and whatever the Father sets in place, certainly does matter!

Unfortunately, Abraham's next-door neighbors have no recognition whatsoever of the One we may call Abba, nor have they any sensitivity whatsoever to the information the Almighty left for us in His Good Book.

In fact the political sovereignty over the Temple Mount within Jerusalem—if not Jerusalem itself—is unequivocally the globe's most unbreakable impasse from now on into eternity, with 1.3 billion Muslims tugging on one end of the rope, and the thus-far unnumbered stars of the sky and sands of the seashore digging in on the other. And then there is the Ancient of Days with gavel in hand somewhere in the mix! It makes an interesting vision!

And that's what made the likes of Yasser Arafat and Saddam Hussein—may they rest in *place*—go bonkers at some four Scriptures in our Bibles, including that initial pledge to Abraham:

> *On that day the* LORD *made a covenant with Abram and said, "To your descendants I give this land, from the river of Egypt*[6] *to the great river, the Euphrates. . . ."*[7]

Moreover, the three other texts that equally project Israel's prophetically preset boundaries in a Messianic Age are Psalm 72:8, 1 Kings 4:21, and 2 Chronicles 9:26. What is more, in ten additional supporting references, the covenants of the Lord are declared permanent and nonnegotiable.

Thus, it is ironic that both Yasser Arafat and Saddam Hussein were paranoid about these declarations in the Holy Writ while large percentages of both Christians and Jews neither accept their validity nor even know they exist.[8]

This may be an appropriate time, as well, to remind my current readers that the last eight pages of *Nineveh*, subtitled *The Hidden Harvest*, are a preview, if not an alternate overview, into *Genetically Modified Prophecies*. These pages could be extremely helpful for a review at some opportune point.[9]

The Dilemma of Demographics

Long before Independence, when the Jews began to move back to their ancient homeland in the late 1800s, it was a fairly empty land, according to Mark Twain and other historians;[10] but it didn't take long before an ebb tide of Arabs from all across the Middle East began to flow in, as well.[11] Don't forget the likes of Arafat the Palestinian, who was actually an Egyptian! And that entire influx was particularly of the orientation that preferred Pharaoh's final solution for Jews—not to mention Adolf Hitler's or even Ahmadinejad's.

It should be obvious that not much has changed over the ages because the tug-of-war is of spiritual scope and hardly carnal. The latter can be solved by land or lucre and the like. The former will not be bought or sold, but reflects a Creator's vested interest in His Plan. There always seems to have been a mentality that doesn't care much for the Jews, but even as the old prophet Balaam rejoined when pressured by the King of Moab to curse the Jews:

> *"How can I curse those whom God has not cursed? How can I denounce those whom the LORD has not denounced? From the rocky peaks I see them, from the heights I view them. I see a people who live apart and do not consider themselves one of the nations. Who can count the dust of Jacob or number the fourth part of Israel? Let me die the death of the righteous, and may my end be like theirs!"[12]*

Thus, except for most of the nearsighted international leaders on the world stage—and even a few too many of Israel's own leaders at home—it is no secret that since the UN narrowly granted Israel the right to return to their ancient homeland in 1948, Jihadic venom (aka

Amalek's[13] agenda) has been out with a vengeance to destroy Jacob. Since her rebirth as a nation, Israel has had to fight at least six wars for survival, plus two intifadas. Is there even a difference in the semantics? And more historic hatred is still slithering on the doorstep for 2012.

So at this point, to appreciate the backdrop of demographics—population balance—we must catch the scene of 1948. Immediately on the UN's granting of Israel's Independence, seven Islamic armies poised for her annihilation swept upon her.

No one thought a total reversal could ever happen, but it did. Israel had no operational army in place to defend herself. But Israel's Creator was a God who had a Plan. Israel won! It was interesting. The secular side of Israel even got a bit spiritual for a few days!

But something else also happened in 1948 that has been misreported, misrepresented, and falsified. The Arab—i.e., Islamic—leadership had told their people there was going to be a nasty war; they should get out immediately or be killed by those evil Jews. They said that within six months the Jews would be driven into the sea, and the refugees could all come back to their homes. But of course, that never happened!

When the Arabs attacked Israel again in 1967, Israel again won against all odds. The refugees, still scorned by their Islamic brethren, fled once more from the "West Bank" primarily, to Jordan. When Jordan finally got fed up with Arafat's Palestinian pawns, he took them farther north into Lebanon. We might again note, the Palestinians are a *mixture* of Arabs, and were never popularly accepted in any one Arab nation. Pawns will be pawns![14]

Those shelved in Lebanon today have multiplied from 600,000 to some 5 million, and the Palestinian Authority is working 24/7 to press these "refugee pawns" back into Israel. It's hardly for compassion—but at long last to crush Israel with demographics and therefore finally and "democratically" drive the Jews into the sea, as was the initial war-cry back in 1948!

So demographics has now become the new name of the game.

Warfare was the preferred route to genocide of the Jews back in 1948, 1957, 1967, and 1973, but Israel always won! Nevertheless those strongholds of vengeance don't go quietly. Now the label recently has been changed to *Lawfare* or to find a devious trap to "legally" drive the Jews into the sea—at last! But in such mischief as to demographic jihad juggling, there's a bit more research that I might yet mention.

Many of Israel's secular leaders have been worried about a future illicit fudging of Israel's boundaries by flooding the status quo with "democratic" Palestinian votes that could lead to the only "democratic" state in the Middle East (Israel) to be forced to "democratically" commit "democratic" suicide—I already told you earlier in the chapter, this democracy bit was a Greek idea!

Whereas God could see the ins and outs of democracy from all sides, the Greeks couldn't! They thought it was such a good idea everyone would buy in to it. Unfortunately, Aristotle never read the Koran in Arabic to note that "peaceful" pauses in dialogue only have the value to eventually cut down your enemy when he's not looking. Nor has the West caught on to the game to this day! Democracy only works when all participants agree on what is *fair*!

So how do you define *fair* in Arabic? Ah yes, it couldn't mean "impartial"—there is no such word. It must mean "light-skinned"!

So as you can appreciate, this demographic debacle has been political panic to Israel for a while now. Moreover, another look at the threat to bring 5 million simulated refugees down from Lebanon and environs to flood Israel with terrorists isn't exactly brilliant. So to the few backbones yet in Israeli politics—and even less in the EU and the UN—well, it better not happen!

The good news is that the Almighty still hasn't modified His original Plan! And a verification of that is that the researchers who have been monitoring the demographic balance that now exists in Judea and Samaria indicate that it is nowhere near what the prophets of doom have been sobbing. According to annually improving statistics, neither will there be a major shift in the TFR (True Fertility Rate) of either Jewish or Arab women. No changes soon!

Now this is hardly a mundane matter of politically incorrect prejudice. It rather points to a stealthily contrived plot to wheedle away at the promised inheritance of Abraham's turf in the Jihadic struggle for sanctified supremacy in the Middle East. It is crystal clear to all who watch, this has *nothing* to do with human tenure to houses or land. But it has everything to do to get those Jews—at long last—into what? . . . into the Mediterranean Sea for good!

We could add volumes to this demographic tussle alone, but that would take us well out of bounds in time as well as focus on where we are heading.

But we will yet look at the titles of three articles on the struggles for Israel's survival population-wise, including a topic sentence from each. Israel, of course, personifies the Most High's master plan of the Ages, using a chosen Family and her unique Mashiach to usher in an ultimate global redemption.

The first one is: "Israeli Arabs: Modernity Up, Birthrate Down" by Adam Reuter.[15]

A dramatic decline in Israeli Arab fertility rate has been observed during the last 15 years . . . secular Jewish fertility rate has surged, while the number of Israeli Arab births has stabilized in 1995-2009, to around 39,000 annually. Simultaneously, and in contrast to previous demographics, the annual number of Israeli Jewish births surged by 50% from 80,400 to 121,000. Jewish births rose to 69% of total births in 1995, 74% in 2006 and over 75% in 2009.

The balance totally refutes what the scaremongers had been telling us. Another report is: "It's Demographic Optimism . . ." by Analyst Yoram Ettinger.[16]

In 2010, a surge in the Israeli Jewish fertility rate is a long-term, unique, global phenomenon . . . as fertility rates decline sharply in the Third World in general and in Muslim countries in particular. In 2010, there was a 66% Jewish majority in 98.5% of the area from the Jordan River to the Mediterranean (i.e. excluding Gaza). . . .

The left is still fudging. Abba has the situation quite under His control! And a third article is: "Demographic Bogey" by Moshe Arens.[17]

> Those Israeli advocates of a "two-state solution" who trumpet a demographic peril to Israel, may have had a few restless nights after perusing the latest demographic report released by the Central Bureau of Statistics as a New Year began. As claimed by Yoram Ettinger for the past few years, it turns out that the demographic demon is not what it's cracked up to be. Now it's official. Demography seems to be working in favor of the Jewish population.

Home-grown secular scare tactics scurry to the paranoia of giving the Promised Land back to Baal. Don't believe it!

All three reports can be reviewed in the endnotes plus two other research articles,[18] which may be of added interest. All flow directly into the King of the Universe's Genetically Modified prophesied promises for eternity.

Therefore, in this chapter as we are closing in on finalizing my cryptic conception of Genetically Modified Prophecies, may we take one more brief overview of where we are heading.

We welcomed the 7,000 Bnei Menashe wanderers who have found their way back into their promised land, only to be hopefully joined by yet to be measured multiples of unknown millions more who yearn to approach their own long-promised portals.

Yet the chapter has been both a perimeter of potential, countered by a hard core stronghold of a resurrected Amalek[19] struggling to buttress Jerusalem with protégé Arafat's "million martyrs" threat of the not-too-distant past. Those who know the King of Creation hardly question the outcome, but as fury rages, nothing reveals the vitriolic venom across millennia better than veteran author Joseph Farah's classic article on: "Too Many Jews."[20] Farah exposes bias from internecine jealousy beginning with Cain and Abel on into untold rivalries across the breadth and depth of Scripture. Consider:

Too Many Jews

"**Too many Jews.**" That was the comment former President Jimmy Carter scrawled on a memo suggesting prospective members of the board of the Holocaust Memorial Council.

"**Too many Jews.**" That was the problem Carter saw with the names suggested by Monroe Freedman, executive director of the council, he revealed in a stunning interview with WND's Jerusalem bureau chief Aaron Klein this week.

"**Too many Jews.**" Naturally, Freedman was shocked by the statement given the Holocaust Memorial Council's job was to establish the Holocaust Memorial Museum in Washington. The Nazi Holocaust took the lives of approximately 6 million Jews during World War II.

"**Too many Jews.**" "If I was memorializing Martin Luther King, I would expect a significant number of board members to be African American," explained Freedman. "If I was memorializing Native American figures, I'd expect a lot of Native Americans to be on the board."

"**Too many Jews.**" What prompted Freedman, a "self-proclaimed liberal" like Carter, to speak out years later on the comment was the release of Carter's book *Palestine: Peace Not Apartheid*, which strongly suggests Israel's "intransigence" is responsible for the Middle East conflict.

"**Too many Jews.**" Ultimately, that's what Carter and others like him believe is the real problem in the Middle East: too many Jews. There are about 7 million Jews living in Israel, nearly 1 million of them refugees from predominantly Muslim Arab lands populated by 300 million non-Jews.

"**Too many Jews.**" It is this usually unspoken belief that leads to ethnic cleansing policies like we see completed in the Gaza Strip, from which all Jews have been forcibly removed—from barren lands they had settled peaceably and turned into gardens. The same kind of "no Jews allowed" policies will soon lead to the forcible evacuation of Jews from historically Jewish lands in Judea and Samaria.

"Too many Jews." But, of course, those policies will never be enough for the Jew haters of the world, people like Jimmy Carter and the terrorists he defends in the Palestinian Authority. There will always be "too many Jews" as long as Jews are permitted to live in the Middle East, their historic and enduring homeland. . . . [Truncated, see website][21]

"Too many Jews." That's what Jimmy Carter believes is the problem. That's what Hamas believes is the problem. That's what Hezbollah believes is the problem. That's what Mahmoud Abbas believes is the problem. That's what Syria and Iran believe is the problem. And, of course, that's what Hitler believed was the problem.

"Too many Jews." How ironic that we would find out the truth about Jimmy Carter because of his meddling in the effort to memorialize Hitler's victims.

"Too many Jews."

So as we noted earlier in this chapter, with Jerusalem metaphorically still on Center Stage back to the farthest seat in the balcony, Abba still runs the show! And Abraham, complete with Y chromosome, still holds the lead role! Perhaps enough has been noted of Jimmy Carter for your adequate consideration of his mentality, except that the King of Moab probably served a lot longer than Carter's four-year presidency; but even then, he had much more to learn about messing with the Jews as we noted in endnote xii.

So may we move on to our final chapter and pick up, not on what the kings of the earth might presume, but what the Ancient of Days has to conclude on His end-of-days projection for Abraham's family.

CHAPTER 13

The Line Below the Bottom Line

Perhaps we might suggest again that the bottom line for our purposes in pursuing those promises to Abraham across time, is that we reconsider that key Scripture as we began Chapter 2:

> *"However, the days are coming," declares the LORD, "when men will no longer say, 'As surely as the LORD lives, who brought the Israelites up out of Egypt,' but they will say, 'As surely as the LORD lives, who brought the Israelites up out of the land of the north* [i.e., **the lands of idolatry**], *and out of all the countries where he had banished them'"* (Jeremiah 16:14–15).

And again may we recall that as in most languages, many words may have multiple meanings depending upon the context. And the insights we gained in Chapter 2 were that "north" may hardly be exclusive to a compass point, but rather to a symbolism of the idolatry of the Baal-worshiping Canaanites on Mount Saphon—*Mount Tzaphon* (i.e., *Mount North*) in Hebrew.

And that analogy of "north" must indeed encompass all end-of-days global rebellion from bowing the knee to *anything*—materialism, affluence, political power, self-styled freedom, hedonism, and all manner of humanism. It includes that gamut of self-glorification that rebuffs any and all supremacy of a Sovereign God over His Creation.

The King is hardly that mocking manufacture of Elvis after all! It's Elohim[1]—and bowing to *anything* in conflict with the King of Creation might just as well be expressed as *everything*!

Now that's not a bad bottom line of identity for Abraham's posterity. But the disheartening news these days is the dwindling commitment from Abraham's family of former times, and that would also include the decline of those seriously committed candidates of Abraham's admirers from across the nations who may be still left standing up. Of course, we should allow that in suggesting *casual* candidates there might be legion, but the catch-22 is that *seriously committed* bit. These days that's a tad harder to come by. But may we read on to detect that if somehow, there could yet be a brighter ray of hope after all?

Perhaps we're now getting a bit closer to any consideration of what yet could possibly be *below* a bottom line? Maybe not only what it is, but what can we do about it? The Jews might see the shortfall as yearning for redemption—whereas the understanding among the Goyim[2] may alternatively be a cry for revival.

If you ask the participants, however, this might involve a not-so-grand canyon of unbridgeable arguments that lead nowhere but to the bottom of the chasm. But as a linguist, a sometime counselor, and a friend across many facets of so-called faith-factions, I'm not so sure that there's not a good deal of overlap between the two expressions above.

So am I hinting that there is more than one recipe for righteousness? No way! I didn't say that, nor do I believe it! Rather, it's Abba who has the sovereignty to do exactly what He said and carry out exactly what He planned with awesome expertise—and without asking Aristotle or even Constantine for advice!

However, that line of control below the bottom line shouts that the major consideration must lie elsewhere like personalized, self-styled agendas perhaps, that must be reprogrammed a bit—Jew or Gentile!

If any selection for qualifying as a pebble on Abraham's beach calls

for Aristotle's sieve of humanistic performance, forget that one immediately!

Or if you also need Big Brother's[3] handy home monitor to keep an
eye on the crowd across the corridor, forget that, too! Fast!

Therefore, is performance—good, bad, or otherwise—irrelevant?
Hardly! Proverbs 28:9 is clear:

> *If anyone turns a deaf ear to the law* [aka "the Torah" in Hebrew],
> *even his prayers are detestable.*

As well as Proverbs 16:2:

> *All a man's ways seem innocent to him, but motives are weighed by*
> *the LORD.*

Will a Woman Surround a Man?

As I was working through an earlier chapter, I came across that
frequently quoted—most likely misquoted—text in Jeremiah 31:21–22
about the Most High doing a "new thing," which could include misap-
plication on anything from goodies for the greedy to prosperity for the
parishioners. Here it is:

> *"Set up road signs; put up guideposts. Take note of the highway, the*
> *road that you take. Return, O Virgin Israel, return to your towns.*
> *How long will you wander, O unfaithful daughter? The LORD will*
> *create a new thing on earth—a woman will surround a man."*

The "new thing" bit often ends up in the hamper for hopeful happenings; however, other more serious theologians attribute that latter
segment as a reference to virgin birth, which I also must reject out of
hand—not on the basis of theology but linguistics. That's a long way
from what it really says!

Of twelve variant translations of Jeremiah 31:21–22, four of them
express the NIV rendition "surround a man" as "encompass a man";
three drop the /en/ and say ". . . compass a man"; two others translate it

". . . protect a man"; one says ". . . encircle a man"; and one more, a foot-note in the NIV, suggests ". . . go about seeking a man."

This last rendition is getting closer because what must be the crown jewel of all twelve of these seemingly toss-of-the-dice efforts, the *New Living Translation*, expresses it like this:

> *"Set up road signs; put up guideposts. Mark well the path by which you came. Come back again, my virgin Israel; return to your towns here. How long will you wander, my wayward daughter? For the* LORD *will cause something new to happen—**Israel will embrace her God**."*

The *New Living* rendition, of course, also shouts from the house-tops in underlining our final direction and ultimate conclusions of our Genetically Modified journey.

I shared the above dartboard dilemma with our publisher, and he didn't say, "crown jewel." That was *my* label. He responded, "You've struck gold!"

And he sent me two more translations of these same two verses that I had not seen: *The Common English Bible* speaks the most pre-cisely:

> *"How long will you hem and haw, my rebellious daughter? The* LORD *has created something new on earth: **Virgin Israel will once again embrace her God!**"*

And the *Message Bible* graphically paraphrases it as:

> *"Set up signposts to mark your trip home. Get a good map. Study the road conditions. The road out is the road back. Come back, dear virgin Israel, come back to your hometowns. How long will you flit here and there, indecisive? How long before you make up your fickle mind? God will create a new thing in this land: **A transformed woman will embrace the transforming God!**"*

Three clear biblical witnesses for Israel's homecoming to Mashiach are good enough for me! I think we've already established that translating from Hebrew to Greek or English may have a few problems! But I've bent over backward—and more—to underline that this book is *not* only about Israel's meeting her Mashiach. It's about my—our—meeting Israel's Messiah—Mashiach—as well! There are not two Messiahs but one and only one, no matter how many ways there are to spell it!

The woman is not any woman but Israel, and the male gender she embraces is not any man but the end-of-days representative of God Himself, Israel's Mashiach.

But what about our two or three principle that sets the stage for resounding truth over against one isolated idea on a meaning that matters? We have it! The book of the Prophet Hosea is replete with the representation of a wayward wife coming home! Hosea 3:4–5 spells out the identical concept:

For the Israelites will live many days without king or prince, without sacrifice or sacred stones, without ephod or idol. Afterward the Israelites will return and seek the LORD their God and David their king. They will come trembling to the LORD and to his blessings in the last days.[4]

So Who's Got All the Answers?

But hold it—Jew or Gentile—before anyone gets any funny ideas of either defensive or offensive recoil to the above shame-on-you-Israel scenario involving the Tanakh prophets—not one word of what I have written can belong exclusively to either side of the two households of holiness.

Anyone who presumes to know one jot or tittle of the Good Book must know that neither Jew nor Goyim has one harried hope of heading heavenward without Abraham's search engine—actually Abba's. The Jew is central—and always has been—to the Father's plan.

So when the Holy Writ says Israel, that's all of us in this thing together. And when it says "last days," we're all getting closer to that together. So let's all listen up a bit!

As I began in Chapter 1, this book is not about how to successfully pass the Pearly Portals. I would presume that most of my readers have either passed that point or are actually hopefully headed in that direction.

In the case of the Great Divide, there is one only Bridge to get across. Jacob saw it in his classic dream in Genesis 28:10–22, and "*knew it not*" until it was all over.

Moses was mentored by the Most High from the Burning Bush to the top of the Mountain and then wrote us five study books for our own homework!

And the First-Century Faithful also became privy to the Plan. Though I can't vouch too happily on what happened after that, but it's in some of my other books and bulletins.

Moses also told us to ever keep our eyes open for any future insight in Deuteronomy 18:15:

> "*The LORD your God will raise up for you a prophet like me from among your own brothers. You must listen to him.*"

But unfortunately, some on both sides of Abraham's family tend to have a tad of sibling rivalry. *That moment of truth below the bottom line is, What do we do next?* We'll get to the fine print shortly, but I suggest setting up a communication channel with Abba and don't turn your iPod off! Let me tell you this right now: Both branches of Abraham's benefactors have a few problems, and I refuse to be the arbitrator. And if you're wise, you won't try it either. Abba still keeps the gavel!

For the Goyim, remember that Hebraic Roots run deep into Eden's lush black earth, while Western roots likely lie shallow in Europe's lumpy clay of Rome's neo-legalism. Careful!

The Jew may not have been the brightest light in that hallway supposedly skirting past idolatry, and their factions of friction do abound, but it's nothing like the some 500 splinters of Goyim denominational factions that fracture the faith of all those other professed faithful followers of truth.

And for one and all, if democracy is your destiny down here, and if doctrine is your deity, or if tradition is what lights your halo—there may be some problems. Remember—there is an Abba who wants your intimacy not your intelligence—which may not be much of a bargain to strike anyway! After all, He's not naïve!

Never forget: It's not what we profess but whose ear we actually possess! There's no substitute for good communication with the *Ruach Ha Kodesh*—the Holy Spirit.

Taint Nuthin' What Ya Thought!

Apologies to my readers in the UK because the above heading is actually in *genuine* English! Its translation was divulged to me by a brilliant doctor friend of mine, whose bilingual expertise speaks an alternate dialect of English out of the state of Georgia, USA. But this homespun Georgian expression carries so much clout that I couldn't resist using it for the long-awaited arrival of Mashiach by both Jew and Gentile. I'll keep to the Hebraic spelling out of respect, since He will be undoubtedly more fluent in Hebrew than English!

But presupposing this much anticipated high point of history, a queue of "I told-you-so's" could well be expected to be lined up on either side of the Jordan River—political temperaments permitting—and in both directions. But His appearance will hardly be to settle nasty scores of personal agendas that have lasted 2,000 years—more or less. But I'm predicting that there will be no heading as apropos for the arrival of Mashiach as *"Taint nuthin' what ya thought."* For Jew, Gentile, cynic, or Calathumpian—it just can't be exactly what anyone might have imagined.

Indeed it *will* be different! And for one and all—again on both sides of the Jordan—who passionately persist in an I-told-you-so agenda may be strangely silent—some perhaps for the first time in a long while! That should even add to the interest! The King of the Universe is not to be blasphemed with the mentality of Hollywood Oscars or the Melbourne Cup!

If we can believe the prophets, either before or after the long-incoming event, there will be massive, down-to-earth upheaval for sure—wars and rumors of wars, earthquakes, and famines! Rumblings are already rife. And the humanist die-hards who are rarely rational are even already out and about to make a few final bucks amid the brilliance on gimmicks like "famine insurance"! Some people just don't get it.

But there is always a bit of good news. Before the promised New Heaven and New Earth, I also seriously predict an escape hatch for anyone holding a Psalm 91 voucher![5] And there will certainly be some awe throughout the following transition to better times. Moreover, a bit of comfort to the heretofore hassled—I very seriously doubt there will be all that much arrogance to put up with—within earshot of Mashiach at least!

Moreover, those of you whom I have been consistently considering thus far as I write, are actually those of us who have some inkling of what this "sand and stars" bit is all about. Unfortunately, there are jillions who neither know nor care. Now it's certainly not that I am calloused for the welfare of the confused, but after all I must diligently get through to you, my readers, first. And for all the rest, we can only cross that bridge when we get there!

Metaphors of sand and stars they may be, nevertheless peering through the opposite end of the telescope, a relationship with their Designer is far more significant. So where do we look next? For sure, the Messiah, aka Mashiach!

Our Jewish friends strongly believe that when Mashiach (Hebrew) finally arrives, it will be a first-time event. New Testament adherents—predominately Gentile—on the other hand, believe Messiah (Greek-English) will be on a return ticket. So what's the next step?

Back to That Bedrock

But for now, it's time we pick up a tad of added insight on that seeming afterthought: "*the line below the bottom line.*" What illusive concept have we coined with this *Genetically Modified Prophecy* anyway? This title wasn't dreamed up in a vacuum, nor without a bit of serious searching for biblical answers on what's going on and where we are at in Kingdom Plans.

At this crucial point for clarity and understanding of this entire probe into Hebraic genetics, we must review once more the multinational track on which we have come, beginning *even before* Abraham. If you know your Bible, earthly Eden precedes Heaven, Cain precedes Abel, Ishmael came before Isaac, Esau paved the way for Jacob, and the breakdown of Babel eventually heralded the re-gathering of Abrahamic genetics. That's seemingly back to front, and if we consider Hebraic worldview, night precedes day!

If—as research has it—the male of the species carries the Y chromosome[6] that ultimately defines his posterity, then Abraham's *offspring* would have had the potential to play catch-up in *any* Hebraic community established even before his time in places like China, or even after the Babel breakup. And it is the *females* of any and all surrounding cultures who carry the babies—many of whom will be carrying the Y chromosomes in the males. Remember, we went through this potential back in Chapter 3? And the potential of the sand and stars multiply!

And there were even other options of the catch-up with Abraham's genetics into China from the House of Isaac exiled in Assyria, or even the ancient Silk Road as also listed in Chapter 3. And there was that same Silk Road flowing through Japan, as well.

And there was also the scattering throughout the Pacific Islands following the end of Hebraic slavery in Egypt. Although with much smaller population density, there was a much wider distribution once settlement in the Pacific had begun.

And we continue on with the myriad of communities in Africa, India, and the multitudes of indigenous populations in North America or the Maranos in Latin America, not to mention the massive melting pot of America itself.

Those former communities comprise much of what is understood as Third World today, and I haven't even begun to mention the mixing of genetics throughout Western Asia, Western Europe, the Balkans, and those even more researched havens of traditionally termed "*Lost Tribe*" scattering. We can be sure Abraham's linkage has by now passed by all those venues en masse.

But don't quit thinking now! This final wrap-up is not about merely *Hebraic* linkage across the planet, but *Genetically Modified* linkage throughout the females of these cultures who continue to carry Abraham's Y chromosome to the length and breadth of the Third World. This has opened the floodgates of Abraham's genetic sand and stars—up, down, and throughout the Goyim, aka Gentile world, that has known no barriers! That inclusion gives us a few more galaxies and briny beaches—quite a few—to count on! Abba's no dummy—pretty clever with those prophecies!

Scripture Stirs the Soup

From Genesis onward, biblically declared interrelationships with the Gentile world—with the cousins, the distant cousins, and even the far-out cousins—were not tucked in a corner. There was Ruth the Moabitess who flowed—fabulously—into the line of Mashiach. Rahab the Innkeeper[7] of Jericho has a similar story.

Moses' father-in-law, Jethro (aka Reuel), and brother-in-law, Hobab, were both Kenites from the sand dunes of Midian, and as such became useful contributions to their kinsfolk by marriage as guides and advisors through the treachery of the desert terrain. Of course these in-laws were a minor but measurable part of the "*mixed multitude*"[8] that accompanied the Hebrews into the wilderness—adoptees, as it were. The *NIV* suggests "*many others.*" Sadly in the long run, the Midianites[9] eventually became notoriously naughty in later years by lining up with Moab to deliberately do in their fellow desert wanderers, and again in attacking Israel in the days of Gideon,[10] but the door was always open to the neighbors who behaved themselves!

Most mixtures had far more favorable outcomes. Moses' wife was also a Midianite. Joseph's wife was an Egyptian, yet her sons, Manasseh and Ephraim, inherited some of the highest non-Hebraic recognition of all. To her two sons was divided Joseph's "double blessing"—the leadership of *two* of Israel's twelve tribes. And both tribal princes were therefore half-Egyptian!

And then there was ever commendable Caleb the Kenizzite, the high-profile hero of Hebron, who was assimilated into the tribe of Judah.

If Caleb's energies at eighty-five years[11] made him the most admirable non-Hebrew adoptee into the Tents of Abraham, there was one other traditional Hebrew who might register a witness for spreading the potential of the promises to the Patriarch for perhaps the farthest reaches back in those days.

Unless you're from Hollywood, it could be a bit embarrassing on today's Judeo-Christian hierarchy of values, but Solomon's 1,000 wives and concubines—predominately non-Hebraic—obviously did their bit to unwittingly, yet sovereignly, roll out the Designer's blueprint of Abraham's Y chromosome!

I'll let you think that one through before we go on!

Abba's Communication Channel

Therefore, with all seriousness to share in a worldwide opportunity to hear the Father's heartbeat—to actually know the Abba of Abraham as the Patriarch himself once intimately knew—may we modify our mindset to catch the cues for global calamities yet to come. Let us perceive those looming disasters paralleling the Great Flood, sense the divine authority to curtail Babel's tallest tower, or from earthquakes we have known,[12] being privy to the potential power of a devastating shaking yet to come? Or may we note an Abrahamic value system of which he nodded his assent to the Almighty? Or do we humanistically dismiss such "nonsense" as mere passing thunder?

If his genetics are going global—or have gone global—in plain ordinary people like you and me, is it possible that we might be able to brush up a bit with our communication skills heavenward? Why not? It happens all the time. Abba has forever had His ways and means to communicate with the ordinaries. An "ear to the ground" is not nearly as brilliant as an ear to Heaven!

So make no mistake. It's hardly through Abraham, dead or alive. He's just one of the ordinaries, as well. If we have the Abrahamic heritage—and it looks like a fair few of us do—Abba has the means to connect—hardly through Abraham—but through His *Ruach*[13]—His Holy Spirit.

This is precisely the exact time for a simple clear-cut question on what I'm thinking about when I start talking about something *below* bedrock—the line *below* the bottom line.

The core root we considered in Jeremiah 16 (back when we began Chapter 2) is what Heaven and earth understands in the significance of Abraham's Family coming out of Egypt (slavery I) *versus* what Heaven and earth *will comprehend* when that same Family—plus another "mixed multitude" with a jillion more Goyim[14]—comes out of idolatry (slavery II).

Better read that again carefully.

Our bedrock has been two enslavements of Abraham's Family. The first was out of Egypt—back then. The second is out of idolatry plus massive Gentile add-ons—now! The Ruths, the Calebs, the Jethros, and the Rahabs—and the end-of-days Christian Zionists—have never quit coming!

And the line below the bottom line is what are we to do—Jew or Goyim, individually or together—with this Genetically Modified phenomenon?

The obvious answer at this point is nothing more or nothing less than simple ongoing communication with the Designer of Destiny. And if you don't have good reception at the moment, the smartest thing is to tune up your set!

For many of my friends, there's nothing new here, either. A relationship with the Creator is what we *want*; communication with the Divine Planner is what we *need*. That's all Abraham had. He was prelaw; he was pre-synagogue; he was pre-Church, pre-doctrine, pre-dispensational, and pre-end time fantasies. And he was pre-everything else that smelled of organized religion.

But did he ever have a communication—a partnership—with the Most High! The Scriptures repeatedly state from the Tanakh onward that:

> *Abraham believed God, and it was "credited to him as righteousness."*[15]

Revival, What's That?

Remember my Waola friends from the Papua New Guinea Highlands back in Chapter 5, who had known for centuries that there *was* a God up there somewhere? When they got the word that He *was* still in business, that was a new day for them and their whole tribe. Five decades on—two of those decades being *without* the influence of Western Bible teachers—they have some 130 tribal congregations and around 15,000 believers, and we might conclude that this is something that could be regarded as revival, or in Hebrew "*shuv.*"[16] On the one hand, this is only one of PNG's 830 tribes; but on the other hand, it is not unrealistic to compare it with what has happened across most of the Papua New Guinea nation. It was the Ancient of Days and *not* a Billy Graham who came on front and center stage—and that is hardly to disparage Dr. Graham's own very fruitful ministry!

The term *revival* is more or less of Christian coinage, though the word does occur once in the *New King James Bible* translation of the Tanakh.[17] From discussions with my Israeli friends, perhaps *redemption* might be their nearest Jewish equivalent to *revival* and that in association with Messianic appearance. For that matter, not all Christians use the term in the context of their various expectations or understanding, either. To close this probe into Genetically Modified Prophecies, let me address primarily those who are more comfortable to pray for, plan for, wait on, and hope for an end-of-days awakening. That might be another way to describe it. Let me say in all sincerity, I can and certainly do, identify with some of your expectations.

On the other hand, a few of you don't plan on being here anyway, so I don't have a great deal of advice to offer, except I hope you're not overly naïve, but you can stick around for a few more closing thoughts regardless!

I do hear a lot of well-meaning believers talking up revival, but from what I have noticed in the last two decades across the Third World and around the globe, that too *"Taint nuthin' what ya thought."* Western-styled revival with its flaunt, flash, and commercialism, is no longer what a non-Western world is sold on.

Like my tribal friends in the Papua New Guinean Highland setting, once their ancient legends came to life with a Father who cared, the floodgates opened. Moreover, the recent report of a very similar grassroots phenomenon of non-sectarian faith in Brazil is one additional reflection of Third World hunger for an Abrahamic-mannered relationship with the God of Abraham, Isaac, and Jacob.

Abraham circumcised himself and the males of his household without so much as a *Physicians' Desk Reference*; he bargained with some delicate dickering for the ransom of the entire city of Sodom—but had to concede the lot! Yet in the diciest deal of all, he trusted his Friend to the bitter brink in the proposed sacrifice of his son, Isaac—and that one he won! Now that kind of communication of humans with Heaven is not good enough via dreams, nightmares, or nutcase nuances, and neither I nor multimillions of Bible believers—Jew or Gentile—are prepared to propose that it didn't happen.

So my point is that reasonable talk-back with the Most High is very Abrahamic. Obviously it won't always end in such earth-rending results. I myself have had some fairly meaningful messages, as did our Jewish friend Gershon Salomon in the Golan Heights battle as reported in the amazing anecdote near the end of Chapter 2. Moreover, there have been multitudes of similar reports in the Good Book of mortals with far less status than Father Abraham. And all the while communication with the King of the Universe continues apace—and we will find it especially common place in the Third World. For those who may not believe it, well, that's their problem. For me—been there, seen that!

But my next point is that human genetics has *much* to do—*everything* to do—with this kind of Abrahamic-styled communication with the Creator of the cosmos. When our personally designated DNA cries out for Daddy—plus that which had been genetically modified over the millennia to include the Y chromosome of Abraham into an otherwise Gentile culture—we have a Kingdom setting to hear Abba calling us Home. That might be to the New Jerusalem eventually, but for starters it's just home with Abba wherever that happens to be at the moment. In Exodus 19:3–8 the Israelites are identified with their divine assignment:

". . . out of all the nations, you will be my treasured possession"

This is not some cushy favoritism, the ultimate key to the treasure chest being dangled in the center of the discourse:

". . . if you obey me fully and keep my covenant."

Rather than perks, it's a massive responsibility to reflect the light of Abba to the darkest corners. Some have done their best while others have done their best to run the other way! But this is not our focus at the moment.

Back toward the end of Chapter 2, under the heading "What Jeremiah's Prophecy Really Told Us," we looked briefly at NASA's Deep Space Probe. And I reiterate that the only technology humankind has ever developed is a copy of sorts of what the Creator of the Cosmos began in Genesis 1:1:

"In the beginning God . . ."

Deep Space communication needs a sender and a receiver. And that didn't begin with NASA. It began "*in the beginning.*" The sender was the Ancient of Days Himself. And even though there were others before him, in Genesis 12 a very well tuned-in receiver was our much-mentioned role model, Avram.[18] But Avram-cum-Abraham was hardly exclusive of *all* that sand and stars that followed him! And that, of course, includes all the add-in Goyim—aka Gentiles—from Righteous Ruth to Solomon's surrogates—whoever picks up on Abba's Talk Show. It's been running for a while now, from the Patriarchs, from the Prophets, and also from the Promises. We can see it coming! And there will be exceptionally good reception all across the non-Hellenistic Third World, genetically linked in to Abraham's now divinely extended offspring!

Indeed, that unrivaled revival waiting in the wings for the devastating dust of humanistic rebellion to settle may not be Hillsong any more than Wesley, Bach, or Beethoven, who each have served the scenario of their day. When the gimmicks of Western methodology have given way to a family-styled Third World tsunami of that globally scattered seed of Abraham, those seeds should all blow back from their long-lost search for their Abba God.

In a sort of modified "talkin' in tongues," one last time from Georgia:

"Taint nuthin' what ya thought."

Epilogue: Scriptures Spanning
Our Genetically Modified Study

THE ULTIMATE PROMISE
And so from this one man—and he as good as dead—came descendants as numerous as the stars in the sky and as countless as the sand on the seashore (Hebrews 11:12).

THE DUAL DELIVERANCE OF DESTINY
"However, the days are coming," declares the LORD, "when men will no longer say, 'As surely as the LORD lives, who brought the Israelites up out of Egypt,' but they will say, 'As surely as the LORD lives, who brought the Israelites up out of the land of the north [i.e., IDOL-ATRY], *and out of all the countries where he had banished them.' For I will restore them to the land I gave their forefathers* (Jeremiah 16:14–15).

THE ASSIGNMENT
"I took you from the ends of the earth, from its farthest corners I called you. I said, 'You are my servant'; I have chosen you and have not rejected you. So do not fear, for I am with you; do not be dismayed, for I am your God. I will strengthen you and help you; I will uphold you with my righteous right hand. . . . For I am the LORD, your God, who takes hold of your right hand and says to you, do not fear; I will help you. Do not be afraid" (Isaiah 41:9–13).

THE COVENANT HOMELAND
On that day the LORD made a covenant with Abram and said, "To your descendants I give this land, from the Wadi of Egypt to the great river, the Euphrates" (Genesis 15:18).

MOAB'S MOMENT OF TRUTH
"How can I curse those whom God has not cursed? How can I denounce those whom the LORD has not denounced? From the rocky

131

peaks I see them, from the heights I view them. . . . Who can count the dust of Jacob or number the fourth part of Israel? Let me die the death of the righteous, and may my end be like theirs!"
(Numbers 23:8–10)

THE FATHER'S DIARY
"I, the LORD your God, am a jealous God, punishing for the sin of the fathers to the third and fourth generations, but showing love to a thousand generations of those who love me and keep my commandments" (Deuteronomy 5:9–10).

THE FATHER'S SHADOW
He who dwells in the shelter of the Most High will rest in the shadow of the Almighty. I will say of the LORD, "He is my refuge and my fortress, my God, in whom I trust." Surely he will save you from the fowler's snare and from the deadly pestilence. He will cover you with his feathers, and under his wings you will find refuge; his faithfulness will be your shield and rampart. A thousand may fall at your side, ten thousand at your right hand, but it will not come near you (Psalm 91:1–7).

Appendix A

What You've Always Wanted to Know about DNA but Were Afraid to Ask!

What do a pig, a platypus, and a person have in common? Apart from the letter *P*, the answer is: DNA. These three species have nearly identical genetic makeups. Yet, plain old common sense tells us as we stare at these three that they are as different as, well…a pig, a platypus, and a person. Why is this so?

The simple explanation is as follows: Most living beings are made up of trillions of cells. The average cell is composed of 6.7 x 10^{27} atoms—that's 67 with 26 ZEROES after it! Every one of those atoms are placed in a particular sequence so as to create 1.75 x 10^{14} molecules, which are in turn arranged so that every molecule has a function in both the appearance and purpose of that cell. When you combine all those trillions of cells in a particular sequence, and they are all working in concert with each other, voila! You have a living being. The size, shape, and function of that living being are dependent upon how those trillions of cells are arranged.

What is even more fascinating is…every one of those trillions of cells originally started as A SINGLE CELL or, in the case of mammals, two cells that combined to make one through conception. That single cell then divided and multiplied continuously, morphing into something a little different until it developed various sub-shapes and sizes, and differentiated into organs and tissue types—the brain, the heart, the skeleton, the muscles, and so on. They then combine to produce a LIVING being. This happens over the course of days, weeks, and months.

Now, how do all of these molecules know how to arrange themselves to produce the final result? Here is where it gets even more interesting! All the information for every atom, molecule, cell, and organ is buried deep inside the nucleus of each and every one of those trillions of cells. It's called genetic material. Each species has its own unique genetic material that may be so similar to another species that when you break down this material, the combinations of genes look almost identical—as they are between a pig, a platypus, and a person. However, even the slightest variation in the genetic structure can produce great distinction between species. When it comes to individuals within a given species, the genetic material is so similar as to make it almost indistinguishable. Yet, even within a particular species, there is such an amazing diversity of shapes and sizes.

There are some in the world of science who use this information as evidence for the evolutionary model of life. Time will not allow us to develop that debate much. However, suffice it to say that over the last twenty-five years, more evidence has been produced in the realm of the life sciences that point to a different conclusion to explain inter- and intra-species variation: INTELLIGENT DESIGN. That is, there is overwhelming evidence to suggest that life did not occur by chance, but by design. Two of the many discoveries that have prompted this conclusion are the concept of error minimization and the age of the genetic code. You see, built into the genetic design of each species is a correction mechanism that does not allow for any substantial alteration in its design. This minimizes any error from generation to generation that could create a significant mutation so as to fundamentally alter the species design. Likewise, several very famous origin-of-life researchers have discovered that the age of the genetic code seems to be almost identical to the age of life itself—seemingly negating the theory of progressive evolution and natural selection at least on a grand scale.

Yes, science has climbed the mountain of its own conceit over the centuries only to find Someone standing at the top—a Designer with purpose, focused intelligently on the most miniscule of differences to create such an amazing variety to life!

Here is the bottom line: The information that holds the secret code for the design of every single living being is contained in the genetic makeup of that being—its DNA! And, no matter how many times that being reproduces, whether it is once or a billion times, the instructions originally designed into its genetic material remain *essentially intact* with only very minimal variation. And no matter how similar species may be to one another in their genetic code, there are rules and mechanisms designed into each species' information code that will not allow it to evolve into another species.

One can sort of parallel this with all the grains of sand in the world. Although not truly possible to calculate, someone once ventured to guess that there were 7.5×10^{17} grains of sand on Earth. Yet, each individual grain can be traced back to its origin if analyzed individually: silica, limestone, gypsum, coral, magnetite, etc. So that, whether currently settled on the beaches of Papua New Guinea, the sand dunes of the Negev Desert, the riverbeds of South America, or the lava pits of the Marshall Islands, one can see sand particles that may be of different shapes and sizes, but are identical to others from its origin no matter how far they have traveled to reach their destination.

These notable facts reflect that the creature can never be lost to his species, but a family chain may be forever traced back to its first unit, e.g., the males in Abraham's family forever traced back to the man himself!

Dr. Daniel Robitshek, MD, FHM
Diplomate, American Board of Internal Medicine,
Fellow of Hospital Medicine,
Hospitalist Medical Director, Floyd Medical Center, Rome, Georgia
Past Professor of Medicine, University of California, Irvine & Loma
Linda University Schools of Medicine

Appendix B:
Cultural Observations in the Faiwolmin Tribe of Papua New Guinea

The Faiwolmin people live in another Province some distance from those of the Southern Highland peoples reported in our text, but nevertheless reflect a much similar history indicating an equal potential for ancient Hebraic origins.

1. A high temple had been erected in the village designated to solemnize all ceremonies involving initiation, first fruit dedication, and related ceremonies of sacred significance. The temple was a rectangle by design and set within a surrounding fence likewise rectangular. Only qualified initiates could proceed within the fence, and only a select level of initiates could actually enter the temple (Yol Am) itself. Inside the Yol Am there was an unseen but well-perceived line, and only the high priest dare pass beyond it. A secondary priest just below him was mandated to perform the crucial rites for gardening or hunting. The high priest held his eminent position by inheritance only.

2. A garden had been planted that was used exclusively by the priests, as well as for the first fruit dedication.

3. The Faiwol language has fascinating cognates with Hebrew, of which only a few will be noted here. The Faiwol pluralize with 'im', identical to the masculine noun in Hebrew. Other of intriguing similarity are: /dam/, which means "blood" both in Faiwol and Hebrew; /am/ in Faiwol means "house" or "household," as it likewise alludes to "household of" or "the people of" in Hebrew. In its reference to God, /el/ in Faiwol also carries the concept of "elevated" or "high up."

4. In our earliest days in the community, it was explained to us that some of them were "light" and some "dark." Pigment-wise this may have been of very questionable demarcation; however, we eventually were able to notice three distinct facial features. When it was pointed out to me those whom they deemed were "white" and those they categorized "black," I could see that those who were minimally lighter and

had possibly less actual African features were considered the "light." The real distinction, however, rather than any elusive shade of pigment, was that the side of the clan that was looked to for maintaining the Yol Am priesthood was what they had classified as "light." Indiscernible to us, it had nothing to do with color, but these represented the ethnicity of their ancestors chosen for spiritual seniority! If it wasn't Mosaic, it was getting pretty close!

5. Faiwolmin is but one group of a language family called the Min people. *Min* can mean the people of a certain pre-identified group. They all had similar religious customs, which have now ceased with the advent of Western culture and practice. However, Telefolmin—one particularly prominent area—reportedly had the most holy temple of all. Moreover, their oral tradition had it that all of these "Min" people, of now various languages, migrated from that singular area.

6. My only explanation of these features is, as (the late) Dr. Stephen A. Wurm reported, that there were waves of migration onto the island pushing the earliest migration inland and to the center of the island where the Min people live. If there were Hebrews among them, they may have been few, but seemingly would have had the most influence among the people that migrated with them.

Researched by Charlotte Mecklenburg,
Co-Translator, Faiwol New Testament
Executive Chairperson, Zion Pathways
PO Box 1941, Prineville OR 97754, USA,
Charmeck@gmail.com

Appendix C:
Credibility of Carbon Dating

Having had a long familiarity with the principles of carbon dating, there is one scientific conclusion that can be drawn with certainty: It's less than accurate!

In simplest terms, any and all laboratory measurements must have valid standards of parallel comparison. But carbon dating has had vast variations for comparative measurement for periods prior to the Great Flood, including:

1) Assumptions of the "beginning" ratio of carbon isotope comparisons.
2) Cosmic ray influence across eons of time.
3) Geomagnetic influences across eons of time.
4) Influence of interfering water vapors across those same periods.

The dating by comparative ratios of carbon's two most prominent isotopes—Carbon 12 and Carbon 14—is determined by comparing the number of atomic particles in the nuclei of those two isotopes. That ratio was presumed to be a known constant in the beginning of time—a bit of conjecture for starters!

Whereas the highly radioactive isotopes, e.g., uranium, decay far too rapidly to use for accurate measurement, far more stable Carbon 12 could be a dependable standard. And Carbon 12 comes mixed with a known but extremely minute ratio of Carbon 14. Eventually the less stable Carbon 14 ever so slowly decays (with a half-life of 5,730 years) turning into Nitrogen 14. That is, after 5,730 years, half of it has changed into Nitrogen 14. Thus by comparing it with the original ratio of Carbon 12 to Carbon 14 you can calculate time—sort of! *If* you knew the actual original ratio at Genesis 1:1 and *if* cosmic rays, geomagnetic influences, and the presence of water vapor behaved like what you thought it should do, all is well! But usually these unknowns from back then don't listen to us mortals! This is oversimplified, but should somewhat adequately present the picture.

And there are other comparative theories that abound, but the best that most of us have ever heard was that in those early days there was a cloud envelope—much like Venus today—that circumvented the earth until the Great Flood. Genesis 1 and 2 concur with that concept; it never rained (Genesis 2:5–6) until Genesis 7:11–16, when Noah's family entered the ark and the Lord shut the door. When the Almighty seeded that Venus-like vapor canopy, it all collapsed at once, giving Noah and family witness to their first rainbow as God's Covenant promise in Genesis 9:12–13.

And the credibility of carbon dating went down the gurgler with Noah's run-off!

In my five decades of Scripture translation and rubbing shoulders with the Third World, we learned from Bible society records that there is no culture on earth that does not carry some oral tradition of the Great Flood.

And not only is it apparent that cosmic rays, geomagnetic influences, water vapor, and carbon dating are no longer brilliant benefits for dependable data, but that due to that loss of the foggy vapor shield from cosmic rays, human longevity was cut to 10 percent of what it was—including possible brain damage—since he still assumes that all is well!

So much for carbon dating and related assumptions. If you have trouble with the author's tongue-in-cheek evaluation (mine), you can get even more academically stated appraisals from *Noah's Flood: Birth of the Ice Age* by Robert L. Gielow (Axiom Press); or www.creation-science-prophecy.com (scroll down to Carbon 14 Dating), or a host of other corresponding Creation Science sites.

—*Victor Schlatter, South Pacific Island Ministries, Inc.*

Endnotes

Chapter 1: Abraham's Inheritance of a Promissory Note

[1] Deuteronomy 28:1–13.

[2] James 1:17.

[3] Genesis 17:5.

[4] Deuteronomy 19:15 and five additional references.

[5] Deuteronomy 30:11–14.

[6] Matthew 13:10–17; Mark 4:13–20.

[7] Isaiah 8:14; 1 Peter 2:8.

[8] Matthew 3:9.

[9] Ultrafine unit with dimensions measured in nanometers, nm; billionths of a meter (Wikipedia). Read more at http://www.answers.com/topic/nanoparticle#ixzz1Tfqq85ir.

[10] Luke 11:30–32.

[11] 2 Peter 3:8.

[12] Matthew 24:36.

Chapter 2: No Longer Will They Say, "Out of Egypt"

[1] Victor Schlatter, *Nineveh: A Parody of the Present: Biblical Clues to the Rise and Fall of America* (Mobile, AL: Evergreen Press, 2009), chapter 2, 16–18.

[2] See http://www.pbs.org/wgbh/nova/israel/familylemba.html for a report on the Abrahamic Y Chromosome study among the Lemba in South Africa.

[3] Genesis 11:31.

[4] Psalm 19:1.

[5] Hebrew for the Holy Spirit.

[6] See http://www.templemountfaithful.org/leader.htm.

[7] Holy Spirit as above.

[8] Isaiah 1:2–3.

Chapter 3: Simple As ABC: After Babel—China!

See Genesis 10–11 in general, and Genesis 11:16–26 in particular.

Genesis 11:1–8.

Chan Kei Thong, *Finding God in Ancient China* (Grand Rapids, MI: Zondervan, 2009).

Ibid. See Chapter 3, "Name Above All Names," page 82.

Deuteronomy 19:15; Matthew 18:16; 2 Corinthians 13:1.

E. Raymond Capt, *Missing Links Discovered* (Muskogee, OK: Artisan Publishers, 2003).

Dianna Matsumoto, *The Soul of a Nation* (New York: Master Press, 2009).

Ibid. See pages 133–134, 253, and the similarities of Genesis 1 on page 249.

Chapter 4: Where Did Japan Get Their Omikoshi Ark?
[1] Exodus 31:18 through 32:35.
[2] Matsumoto.
[3] See Endnote 1.
[4] Edwin O. Reischauer, *Japan: The Story of a Nation* (New York: Alfred A. Knopf, 1970).
[5] Matsumoto, 133.
[6] The Kojiki: "Records of Ancient Matters,: 712 AD.
[7] Ecclesiastes 1:9.
[8] See Judges 2:10–19; 3:11; 5:31; 8:28: 13:1, etc.
[9] Exodus 31:18 through 32:35.
[10] Matsumoto, 164, 223.
[11] See http://www5ocn.ne.jp/~magi9/isracame.htm and http://biblemysteries.com/library/tribesjapan.htm.
[12] See www.spim.org.au.
[13] South Pacific Island Ministries, Inc., in 1991.

Chapter 5: How Many Hebrews Left Egypt with Moses?
[1] In-depth discussions of the entire issue can be found under *Musings of Beshallah* that include Rabbis Lawrence Hoffman and Rabbi Maller. See: http://www.synagoguehamptons.org/wp-content/uploads/2011/03/Parshat-Beshalah-January-14-2011.pdf. For another excellent article by the late Rabbi Amichaei Lau-Lavie, see: http://www.facebook.com/topic.php?uid=12091850660&topic=6543. Another valuable URL by Mekhilta De-Rabbi Ishmael is: http://www.answers.com/topic/beshalach#ixzz1Qfnl8VCb.
[2] Gentile.
[3] The language of the Waola tribe.
[4] See Appendix C: The Credibility of Carbon Dating.
[5] Genesis 25:29–34; 27:1–33:20.
[6] Numbers 11:5.

Chapter 6: Just Who Was Avram Pamu?
[1] See www.spim.org.au.
[2] Ibid. Click on "Insights and Articles," Main Menu, Article 8, Victor Schlatter, Port Moresby, *The Post Courier, Weekend Magazine:* "Where Did We Come From?", August 1992, 1.
[3] See Chapter 9: The Longest Road Out of Africa.
[4] Genesis 11:26.
[5] Genesis 17:5.
[6] The Tari Basin is the tribal home of the Hela people.

[7] See www.spim.org.au. Click on "Insights and Articles," Main Menu, Article 8, Victor Schlatter, Port Moresby, *The Post Courier, Weekend Magazine:* "Where Did We Come From?", August 1992, 2.

[8] See Appendix B on the Faiwol and Min people groups for additional parallels of Hebraic reflections among the same 830 tribal cultures and ancient practices of Papua New Guinea.

[9] Now spread to eighty years since that earlier date of the *Post Courier* publication.

[10] Jim O'Malley and Jack Hides, *Papuan Wonderland* (London: Blackie and Son, 1936).

[11] See www.spim.org.au. Click on "Insights and Articles," Main Menu, Article 8, Victor Schlatter, Port Moresby, *The Post Courier, Weekend Magazine:* "Where Did We Come From?", August 1992, 2.

Chapter 7: Vanuatu and Other Far-Flung Islands of the Sea

[1] Victor Schlatter, *Where Is the Body?* (Shippensburg, PA: Destiny Image, 1999), 74–79.

[2] Dr. J. Graham Miller, *Live*, St. Giles Presbyterian Church in Hurstville, NSW, currently out of print. Contact the church library in NSW.

[3] See: http://storiansmol.blogspot.com/2008/09/in-memory-of-rev-dr-j-graham-miller.html.

[4] Genesis 17:1–14.

[5] Matthew 13:10–13.

[6] The Spirit in Hebrew.

[7] Deuteronomy 27:9–26; 28:1–14; 28:15–68, for communal curses and blessings; Exodus 21:17; Leviticus 20:9; 24:15; and Proverbs 20:20 for individual behavior.

[8] Numbers 6:2–21.

[9] Numbers 13:16–17; Joshua 2:1; 1 Samuel 26:4.

[10] Leviticus 15:19–23.

[11] Numbers 27:1–11; 36:1–12 (Zelophehad's daughters).

[12] Joshua chapters 13 through 21; Deuteronomy 19:14; Proverbs 22:28.

[13] Leviticus chapter 18.

[14] See http://www.urielheilman.com/0204palau.html. "A Zionist Message to the South Pacific" by Uriel Heilman.

Chapter 8: The Wrong Place at the Wrong Time

[1] Anton Graceffo. See: http://www.goabroad.net/Brooklynmonk/journals/1715/burma%E2%80%99s-other-karen-tribe.

[2] See Deuteronomy 25:17; Exodus 17:14–15, for example.

[3] Full files of Arabic to English translations by Palestinian Media Watch,

ItimarMarcus, cite references filed by both topic and date, as well as other chapter and verse published references in bona fide "holy writings" that promise just such absurdities! See http://www.palwatch.org.

[4] See historical article on Adoniram Judson's ministry: http://www.answers.cojm/topic/protestantsinburma.

[5] Ibid.

[6] Ibid.

[7] See Chapter 5 in this volume, pages 35-36.

[8] Schlatter, *Where Is the Body?*, 46.

[9] See http://www.answers.com/topic/karen-people.

[10] See subheading "Getting into a Bit More Serious Research" in Chapter 3, page 19.

[11] Genesis 1:1.

[12] Malachi 3:6.

[13] See subheading "Back to Abraham" in Chapter 3, pages 20-21.

[14] Don Richardson, *Eternity in Their Hearts* (Ventura, CA: Regal, 2005).

Chapter 9: The Longest Road Out of Africa

[1] For a parallel significance of a biblical Nineveh, see Schlatter, *Nineveh*.

[2] Ephraim, the younger son of Joseph, who, upon his tribal blessing, was awarded the leadership of one of Jacob's twelve tribes, and was later recognized as the designate head of the Israelite grouping of the ten northern tribes.

[3] Refer to Nova Online/Lost Tribes at http://www.pbs.org/wgbh/nova/israel/familylemba.html.

[4] Genesis 45:10 and 47:27.

[5] See http://en.wikipedia.org/wiki/Great_Zimbabwe.

[6] 1 Kings 9:28 and 1 Chronicles 29:4.

[7] See http://www.pbs.org/wgbh/nova/israel/familylemba.html.

[8] 1 Kings 11:1–3.

[9] Jewish priest.

[10] *Kosher* in this context is not necessarily dietary pattern, but general behavior.

[11] See http://www.amazon.com/Sabbath-Roots-Connection-Charles-Bradford/dp/1578470560.

[12] See http://groups.yahoo.com/group/Sabbath_in_Africa/?yquid=72503.

[13] See Chapter 5, pages 35-36.

[14] See Jeremiah 43:4–11.

[15] Acts 8:27–39.

[16] See http://www.jewishvirtuallibrary.org/jsource/Judaism/ejtime.html.

[17] The Falash Mura is a group of some 8,000 Ethiopian Jews who were forced to convert to Christianity under economic pressures, but now granted the right of return under special permission.

[18] See http://www.time.com/time/health/article/0.8599.1715337.00.html.

Chapter 10: America Was Discovered by Colombo Ben Who?

[1] *Ben* in Hebrew means "son of."

[2] See http://.jewishsa.co.za/upload/file/Chanukah%202009%20-%20JEWISH%20AFFAIRS.pdf, "JEWISH AFFAIRS," Chanukah 2009 Edition, page 40, endnote 60. Cecil Roth interview with Rabbi William Berkowitz, "Why Cecil Roth Believed Columbus Was Jewish."

[3] *Adonai* literally means "Lord." It is a Hebrew substitute word for the actual name of God, which Jews never pronounce. In practice, traditional Jews don't even say "Adonai," because it has become a holy name, as well. They substitute the word *Hashem* (which means "the name"). [Wikipedia].

[4] *Tisha B'Av* is an annual fast day in Judaism, named for the ninth day (Tisha) of the month of Av in the Hebrew calendar. The fast commemorates the destruction of both the First Temple and the Second Temple in Jerusalem, which occurred about 656 years apart, but on the identical Hebrew calendar date. Accordingly the day has been called the "saddest day in Jewish history."

[5] These are average estimates from Wikipedia and others. Between immigration in and Aliya back to Israel, Jewish populations fluctuate continually, nor are they consistent between data suppliers.

[6] See Genesis 15:7.

[7] See http://www.prweb.com/releases/2003/2/prweb56538.php.

[8] Dr. Barry Fell, *Saga America* (New York: Three Rivers Press, 1983).

[9] Dr. Cyrus H. Gordon, *Before Columbus* (London: Lowe and Brydone, 1972).

[10] Fell, 168.

[11] Epigraphic Society Occasional Papers.

[12] Dr. Barry Fell, *Bronze Age America* (New York: Little, Brown, and Co., 1982).

[13] Steven M. Collins, "The American Indians: Early Contacts with Israelites" See: scollins@ll.net, www.bibleblessings.net.

[14] Dr. Fell's publications as noted across the chapter are *Saga America*, *America B.C.*, and *Bronze Age America*. All are also listed with Amazon.com.

[15] Psalm 50:21.

[16] See http://www.ancient-hebrew.org/15_home.html.

Chapter 11: Lost Tribes Fever

[1] The particular blogger is further identified as one pro-Israel Brian Hennessy, not to be confused with his some sixty other current namesakes on Google. However, his focus on potential Hebraic roots represents a multitude from the American Bible Belt and is herein extremely well expressed.

[2] "Can the Ethiopian change his skin or the leopard its spots?" (Jeremiah 13:23).

[3] Exodus 20:5, 34:7; Numbers 14:18; and Deuteronomy 5:9.

[4] Exodus 20:6; Deuteronomy 5:10, 7:9; 1 Chronicles 16:15; and Psalm 105:8.

[5] Deuteronomy 23:3 and Nehemiah 13:1.

[6] Ruth 1:16.

[7] The Bible Belt is the conservative Bible-oriented heartland of America, covering the entire Midwestern and Southern states, stretching from Pennsylvania to approximately the Great Plains.

[8] *Halakah/halakkah*: Talmudic literature that deals with law and with the interpretation of the laws on the Hebrew Scriptures.

[9] See:
www.google.com/search?hl=en&source=hp&biw=1259&bih=878&q=Amish+visit+rabbis+in+Israel&btnG=Google+Search&oq=Amish+visit+rabbis+in+Israel&aq=f&aqi=F&gs_upl.

[10] See: http://www.berlinohioinfo.com/index.php?option=com_content&view=article&id=16&itemid=5.

[11] Arthur Koestler, *The Thirteenth Tribe* (New York: Random House, 1976).

Chapter 12: Seven Thousand More Headed Home

[1] Stephen Epstein, "A Long-Lost Tribe Is Ready to Come Home." See http://www.bneimenashe.com/articles.html. Professor Epstein, Ph.D. Sociology, University of California, Berkeley, is the director of the Science in Human Culture Program and a faculty member at the Alice Kaplan Institute for the Humanities, as well as Northwestern University.

[2] Ibid.

[3] Ibid.

[4] Ibid.

[5] See Abraham as friend of God: 2 Chronicles 20:7; Isaiah 41:8; James 2:23.

[6] The River of Egypt is *not* the Nile, but correctly translated, the Wadi of Egypt just south of the Gaza Strip.

[7] Genesis 15:18.

[8] See again Genesis 15:18, plus three additional references for these same boundaries: 1 Kings 4:21; 2 Chronicles 9:26; and Psalm 72:8. In ten other references, the covenants of the Lord are declared permanent and nonnegotiable. It is ironic that both Yasser Arafat and Saddam Hussein were paranoid about these texts in the Hebrew Scriptures while large percentages of both Jews and Christians neither believe in their accuracy nor even know they exist!

[9] See Schlatter, *Nineveh*, 134–141 for a helpful summary of *Genetically Modified Prophecies*.

[10] Schlatter, *Where Is the Body?*, 61–62, regarding Mark Twain.

[11] See www.spim.org.au, Articles and Insights number 4: "Who Occupies Whose Land?" (December 2002).

[12] Numbers 23:8–10.

[13] *Amalek*: a pseudonym for Esau's hatred against Israel. See Exodus 17:16 and Deuteronomy 25:17.

[14] See http://standpointmag.co.uk/node/4036/full.

[15] Reuter, "Israeli Arabs: Modernity Up, Birth Rate Down."

[16] Ambassador Yoram Ettinger, "It's Demographic Optimism, Stupid!" August 12, 2010. See http://www.ynetnews.com/articles/0,7340,L-3934006,00.html.

[17] Moshe Arens Haarets, "Demographic Bogey," September 14, 2010. See http://www.haaretz.com/print-edition/opinion/demographic-bogey-1.313683#article.

[18] Ambassador Yoram Ettinger, "Demographic Implosion in Moslem Societies," October 17, 2008. See http://www.news1.co.il/Archive/003-D-32561-00.html?tag=18.56-41. Also see Bennett Zimmerman and Michael Wise, "Defusing the Demographic Time Bomb," *In Focus*, March 2008. Bennett Zimmerman and Michael Wise are with the American-Israel Demographic Research Group (AIDRG).

[19] See Chapter 2, Endnote 1. Amalek in real life was a grandson of Esau who led genocidal attacks against Israel in his day.

[20] By Joseph Farah, *World Net Daily*, January 27, 2007. All rights reserved. For full copy, see worldnetdaily.com.

[21] Ibid.

Chapter 13: The Line Below the Bottom Line

[1] *Elohim* is the generic expression for God in Hebrew.

[2] *Goyim* is Hebrew for gentiles.

[3] Refer to George Orwell, *Nineteen Eighty-Four* (New York: Harcourt, 1949).

[4] Beyond the Hosea 3:4–5 reference, Scripture has added reinforcement in Deuteronomy 4:29–30; Isaiah 10:20; and Micah 4:1–2.

[5] Psalm 91:7.

[6] See http://www.pbs.org.wgbh/nova/Israel/familylemba.html.

[7] Some translations name Rahab as a prostitute, but this could be an unkind inaccuracy. She was an innkeeper.

[8] "And the children of Israel journeyed from Rameses to Succoth, about six hundred thousand on foot [that were] men, beside children. And a *mixed multitude* went up also with them; and flocks, and herds, [even] very much cattle" (Exodus 12:37–38 KJV).

[9] Numbers 25:1–15.

[10] Judges 7:1–25.

[11] Joshua 14:6–15.

[12] Revelation 16:18–19.

[13] Hebrew for God's Spirit.
[14] See Chapter 1, Endnote 7 regarding "mixed multitude."
[15] Genesis 15:6; Romans 4:3, 5, 9, 22; Galatians 3:6.
[16] *Shuv* is Hebrew for "return." "Return to God" might therefore be expressed *teshuva*, or "repentance."
[17] The Hebrew Scriptures.
[18] His name was changed to Abraham in Genesis 17:5.

OTHER BOOKS BY VICTOR SCHLATTER

Where is the Body? Discovering the Church in the Heart of Israel
is a wake-up call in these dire days of Israel's restoration and testing, to jar the church into an awakening to God's unique plan of a reborn Israel in an advent of a Messianic Age. It exposes not a few faulty end-time fables that via anti-Semitic bias have feigned honesty in much of the Church. Its aim is reality, truth and above all, faithfully cites the Bible you say you believe.

Showdown of the Gods: The Global Confrontation Between Islam, Humanism and God
ironically went to press on 9-11, 2001, Showdown links ancient Bible prophets to a morally and spiritually decaying globe. It sees daily disasters around us in the light of prophecy, exposing unlikely bedfellows—Islam and New World Order humanism. Both vying for a final crack at a Creator God—at first to feign friendship, finally to draw blood—the nightly news won't surprise old Zechariah!

Who Told You, You Were Naked? From the Fall of Adam to the Rise of the Antichrist
uncovers the naked truth of an unbridgeable chasm between eastern Hebraic and western Greek thinking. You will gain amazing new insight into Media Bias, Humanism, Organized Religion, Political Correctness, and a God-defying New World Order.

Nineveh: A Parody of the Present, Biblical Clues on the Rise and Fall of America
is an overview of waning days as a superpower, by biblically viewing her aside the deeds and demise of 5 ancient kingdoms that have long since descended those trails of no return—Nineveh, Babylon, Persia, Greece and Rome and now post Roman Europe. It's anything but heavy laden history, laced with quips and prickly truth that the Western World must learn.

About the Author

Victor Schlatter spent seven years as a nuclear scientist before responding to a call from Above to upgrade his career to linguistics and Bible translation. In a South Pacific Stone Age scenario, he translated the Waola Scriptures now in their 6th printing. He found that there is no such thing as a primitive language, since Stone Age Waola has more than 100 endings for every verb. His translation has since generated over 130 tribal congregations with some 15,000 believers across Papua New Guinea.

The Schlatters then reached out in a Pacific-wide ministry tying Isaiah's oft repeated "Islands of the Sea" to the long-foretold Israel reborn. Having made annual trips to Jerusalem since 1988, he has kept up in-depth research of the broiling Middle East countdown, especially as it reflects biblical prophecy. He is Director of South Pacific Island Ministries, represents the International Christian Embassy Jerusalem to the South Pacific Islands, and lectures globally.

He was awarded the Queen's Papua New Guinea Independence Medal in 1975 for recognised service to the Southern Highlands, and was selected for Who's Who in Queensland, Australia in 2007. He is the author of *Where Is the Body?* (translated into Russian, Finnish and Dutch), *Showdown of the Gods, Who Told You that You Were Naked?* and *Nineveh: A Parody of the Present—Biblical Clues to the Rise and Fall of America.* He and his wife, Elsie, currently reside in Australia.

Author contact information:
website: http://www.spim.org.au

General book availability:
spimaust@aol.com, spimusa@gmail.com, www.Amazon.com,
and bookstores everywhere

Contacts in Australia:
icejaus@bigpond.com, adminaust@bridgesforpeace.com.au

Contacts in Israel:
www.galileeexperience.com, Emmanuel Bookshop-Jaffa Gate or
Galilee Experience-Tiberias